An A to Z of School Leadership

George Walker

An A to Z of School Leadership

Published September 2007

International Baccalaureate
Peterson House, Malthouse Avenue, Cardiff Gate
Cardiff, Wales GB CF23 8GL
UNITED KINGDOM

Phone: +44 29 2054 7777
Fax: +44 29 2054 7778
Web site: http//www.ibo.org

The International Baccalaureate (IB) offers three high quality and challenging educational programmes for a worldwide community of schools, aiming to create a better, more peaceful world.

IB merchandise and publications can be purchased through the IB store at http//store.ibo.org. General ordering queries should be directed to the sales and marketing department in Cardiff.

Phone: +44 29 2054 7746
Fax: +44 29 2054 7779
E-mail: sales@ibo.org

British Library Cataloguing in Publication Data available

ISBN: 978-1-906345-00-6

Typeset by Prepress Projects Ltd, Perth, Scotland
Printed and bound by HartleyWilprint, Cardiff, UK

Item code: GD173

For Jenny

Contents

Foreword

George Walker is an educator of exceptional experience and wisdom and he has written a unique compendium about leadership. Drawing on his leadership role in four different schools, and his directorship of the International Baccalaureate, Walker punctures much common nonsense and provides healthy dosages of common sense and uncommon sense. In addition, the book is an invigorating blend of surprises, practical suggestions, and pithy formulas; there is also an Arnoldian tour de force about how it feels to embark on and pursue a challenging quest. Leaders from all sectors of life will profit from this book, and educational leaders will place it on the small shelf of indispensable guides.

Howard Gardner
Hobbs Professor of Cognition and Education
Harvard Graduate School of Education

Acknowledgements

I am very grateful for the editorial advice and encouragement that I have received from Sophie Matta and Katya Vines of the International Baccalaureate. They have helped me to write a better book.

I want to thank Dr Albert Penna, Headmaster of Binghamton High School, New York State, for his helpful suggestions from the perspective of an experienced American administrator.

Finally, I want to acknowledge my debt to my four personal assistants – June Self (The Heathcote School), Jackie Wilmer (The Cavendish School), Jenny Buffle (The International School of Geneva) and Célia Arcos (The International Baccalaureate) – whose professional competence, integrity and sense of humour sustained me during the 30 years that form the background to this book.

George Walker
August 2007

School Leadership

Creating the right culture	Scenting the need	Setting the new direction	Communicating the change	Involving others	Making it happen
A is for Appraisal	**E** is for Environmental awareness	**C** is for Change	**T** is for Transparency	**D** is for Delegation	**M** is for Making things happen
P is for Playing by the rules	**K** is for Key performance indicators	**B** is for Board	**V** is for Vision	**I** is for Interviewing	**J** is for Job descriptions
G is for Generosity	**Q** is for Questioning beliefs	**S** is for Strategic planning	**W** is for Walking the talk	**H** is for Human resources	**F** is for Finance
O is for Optimism	**X** is for xenophobia	**L** is for Learning	**Y** is for Yourself	**U** is for Unacceptable performance	**N** is for Nimbleness
Z is for Zest					**R** is for Risk management

On ne conduit le peuple qu'en lui montrant un avenir: un chef est un marchard d'espérance.

One can only lead by showing the people a future: a leader is a dealer in hope.

Napoléon Bonaparte

This is a personal account of leadership and the selection of the 26 topics to match the alphabet from A to Z is a personal choice, reflecting those aspects of leadership that have meant the most to me.

I have no doubt that others would have chosen differently. But that does not mean my choice is based on personal whim. Leadership is fundamentally concerned with change: taking an organization from where it is now to where it needs to be in the future. That description is deceptively simple because it conceals a number of tough challenges that require the leader to recognize the need for change, to translate that need into a clear sense of direction, to describe and communicate it in a manner that will convince others to lend their support, and then to do things that will actually make it happen. And to make things happen you need a surrounding atmosphere, a culture if you like, of intellectual inquiry that encourages and sustains a belief that things can be done differently and done better.

So I am confident that each of my 26 topics is closely linked to those six basic drivers of change (as shown in the facing diagram):

- creating the right culture
- scenting the need
- setting the new direction
- communicating the change
- involving others
- making it happen.

Let me explain ...

Creating the right culture

On the whole people do not welcome change; they much prefer to remain as they are. Familiarity, and the well-honed competence that comes with it, will compensate even for boredom and frustration, which at least have the merit of being the "devils you know". Indeed, stability and predictability—knowing that this year and next year will not be noticeably different—are factors that have traditionally influenced teachers in their choice of career. The professional challenge relished by the bringers of change is rarely viewed in the same enthusiastic light by those being changed. The latter therefore need extra support and encouragement in their new environment and forgiveness for the mistakes they are likely to make. Above all else, the school needs an intellectually stimulating environment in which important educational issues are topics for frequent debate and in which differences of professional opinion are respected and openly discussed.

So I start with the unassuming and apparently uninspiring **A is for Appraisal** because the leaders who have implemented realistic programmes of appraisal have signalled to their colleagues that they care about them, are ready to listen to their hopes and fears, and acknowledge the primary role of a school's staff in bringing about improvement.

Trust is a key factor in determining our response to the unknown. We are unlikely to embark on any new venture of significant risk—physical, financial or cerebral—without the companionship of someone whom we trust. **P is for Playing by the rules** because that helps to establish an environment of trust in which the head is seen as reliable and credible, not someone who, however strongly tempted, breaks the rules to escape from a difficult situation or to give temporary satisfaction to an influential stakeholder.

G is for Generosity, which, alas, is too often perceived as an indication of human weakness: letting off the hook someone who might have been made to suffer. Forgiveness for mistakes, which is probably the most visible sign of generosity in a school, is a prerequisite in creating a culture of mutual support that will allow new initiatives to take root. I remember a friend in industry who ascribed his boss's career success to the fact that he avoided ever making a serious mistake. But, he added, that is why he remained a manager and never rose to a position of senior leadership.

Much of a leader's thinking takes place in the future, and when I went to Geneva it was the future tense in French that I had to master the quickest. **O is for Optimism** describes a future-oriented quality as optimism has no meaning in the past and very little in the present. But without it, and many are finding it harder and harder to sustain, that beacon of a better future, which underpins our commitment to education and our determination to make it more effective, will be obscured by the plethora of darkening problems that currently affect our society and therefore our schools. So I need to be reminded that when I started as a young science teacher it was fun. The daily experience of working with lively young people and supportive colleagues was intellectually stimulating, professionally challenging and socially rewarding, but I doubt that I noticed much of that because it was also fun. Many years later the word fun sounds trivial, even slightly irresponsible, so instead I have decided that **Z is for Zest**. It's not a bad note to finish the alphabet on.

Scenting the need

Perhaps surprisingly, schools turn out to have a predictable rhythm, pace and momentum. The sometimes scary public manifestations of chaotic playground activity and barely controlled youthful energy hide the reality that under the surface the basic organizational issues run rather slowly. There may be an occasional emergency to deal with, but rather few important decisions need be taken in haste, and hardly any are likely to result in life or death. Some school leaders, despite their best intentions, find their attention diverted to the bustle going on in the corridors; after all, that is where it all seems to be happening. Others are quickly seduced into the reassuringly predictable routine of the academic year, which means that what happened this year will come round again next year, and perhaps then we will get it right. Wise leaders realize that the bustle and the routine is determined by what goes on, invisibly, beneath the surface and they try to scent out ways to change that for the better.

What sharpens those senses? Well, **E is for Environmental awareness** of significant local and national trends. How is the world changing around the school and how should the school respond? It is not surprising that school leaders have often been members of Lions and Rotary Clubs, building up their network of "spies" in the local community. Where is the new housing being built? What is the district's education budget looking like and is it true that another big employer is leaving town? But at the same time (despite every government's emphatic denial) education in the developed world is becoming increasingly centralized so national trends have to be followed just as closely, and I found that most of my useful intelligence came from contacts outside the education system.

If the head is to pick up a scent inside the school that eventually leads to change then something or someone has got to provide it. Very often it comes in the form of feedback about the school's performance, indicating that all is not well. But how do we collect and interpret relevant information and avoid being unreasonably influenced by one unfortunate event, one difficult parent or one unhappy student? That is why **K is for Key performance indicators**–because these measurements have been carefully selected to provide feedback that is truly related to issues that will determine the school's success.

Each of us has professional "no-go" areas: aspects of our work that have been shaped by our values and are no longer open to negotiation. But what can we reasonably say is off-limits? **Q is for Questioning beliefs** because school leaders must be willing to reassess even their most deeply held beliefs, which may have been acquired and shaped by a different environment or in a different age that is no longer connected to the school's needs. Life moves on and, although schools are necessarily rather conservative institutions, they must not be shackled by opinions that have turned from well-researched belief into unsubstantiated dogma.

The sense of independence that produces an effective school can also produce a sense of isolation that quickly destroys the source of good ideas. The dangers contained in this isolation explain why, rather dramatically, **X is for Xenophobia**–because the inward-looking sense of pride and tradition that can build a good school can turn into a destructive resistance to other individuals, communities and ideas that are deemed not to belong. Very often the scent for change comes from precisely these other, apparently alien, organizations.

Setting the new direction

It will surprise no one who has read this far that **C is for Change**. By now the scent has been picked up and something needs to be done. Change is in the air, not just for its own sake or to impress the panel at the head's next job interview, but to recognize two basic truths. The first is a cliché but no less valid for that: the successful organization never stands still. The second is less obvious but perhaps more important: it is precisely at a time of stability, achievement and success that a school needs to start changing but, of course, there is no incentive to do so. Only the successful school has different options for the future; for if the school is in crisis the choice has usually come too late.

When it comes to setting the new direction, school leaders should no longer be on their own because **B is for the Board**–of governors, directors, trustees, whatever–and board members must be satisfied that the change is the right direction to take; after all, it is they who will be accepting the final responsibility for the change. Of course, it may have been their idea in the first place; I am sceptical about the conventional wisdom that draws a clear dividing line between governance and management—most good ideas that take a firm root have shared origins.

The board represents the continuity of the school's development, ensuring that any changes form a logical part of a long-term strategy rather than a series of uncoordinated reactions to unexpected crises or the overambitious aspirations of here-today-gone-tomorrow leaders. **S is for Strategic planning**, which is arguably the most important activity the school, and its community, will ever engage in. According to the textbooks it is a well-documented science, but my experience suggests that it is more a multidimensional art that offers a variety of alternative models.

But there is one area of complete agreement: the strategic plan must never lose sight of what the school stands for—expressed in its mission statement—and if that is not concerned with the quality of the students' education then it is time to ask some awkward questions. That is why **L is for Learning** and why school leaders, whatever their background—in academia, business, the law, the church, the military—must accept primary responsibility for its relevance and quality. Wherever the new direction takes us, every signpost must point clearly to learning that is appropriate for the global citizen of the 21st century.

Communicating the change

Persuading others to follow is the most public dimension of leadership. This is what stereotypical leaders—be they military, religious or political leaders—are expected to do well and to do with great charisma on a podium surrounded by microphones and the eagerly awaiting media. They are persuading you and me to follow them. In schools the process is somewhat less dramatic but its purpose is the same: to convince, to cajole and to sell. You will not succeed in changing anything on your own because you lack the time, the skills and the resources. But even if you have each of them in abundance, the change will not last unless it brings the commitment and ownership of those it most closely affects.

Effective communication is therefore a crucial skill of leadership, but there is much more to this than writing well and speaking clearly. Persuasion grows from an inclination to share information rather than withhold it, to open up debate rather than dampen it down, to build an organization in which nothing is concealed because, in the end, it will most certainly be revealed and in circumstances that will cause the maximum embarrassment. That is why **T is for Transparency**.

Mere communication, however, is not enough; leaders must motivate their followers by presenting an inspiring yet credible picture of how the future is going to be better. **V is for Vision** because that requires both the capacity to make sensible predictions about the future and a passion to influence it for the better. We are talking here not about idle dreams but about difficult, tangible realities, and the true leader is the person who simultaneously has the good idea and understands the way to achieve it.

People's responses vary according to the choice of communication medium. Some will be inspired by a powerful speech, others by a well-reasoned paper. Some will react to a strongly visual presentation, others to a structured debate. Evidence suggests that the more ways in which a change can be communicated, the more likely it is to be adopted. **W is for Walking the talk** because this inelegant phrase describes another, and possibly the most effective, means of communicating a change—being it yourself, becoming its visible embodiment for everyone to see.

Inelegant though it may be, "walking the talk" acknowledges one of the most fundamental truths of education: meaningful communication requires a significant personal investment. Information needs a "tinge of emotion" before it becomes turned into knowledge, and that involves the way you understand yourself. It should therefore be no surprise that **Y is for Yourself.**

Involving others

Fundamental to the successful implementation of change is the active collaboration of those who will be most affected by it. Building understanding and commitment to a project takes place in stages. It starts with communication, but telling must progress to selling, then to sharing, then to engaging thinking and finally to developing thinking. The tipping point comes with sharing, because in the end the successful project will be achieved by the hard work of many people who did not share the original idea, indeed may not even have been around at the beginning.

The process of sharing, welcoming and developing other people's ideas, creating ownership rather than alienation, depends upon sharing power and responsibility. It means giving to others the authority and the necessary resources to act and holding them accountable for those actions. Thus, **D is for Delegation**, one of the biggest tests of leadership—the ability to hand over the wheel.

Delegation, however, presupposes that the appropriate people are available to accept new and demanding responsibilities. There is little purpose in involving others when they manifestly lack the required knowledge, skills and experience. The recruitment of high-quality staff is an enviable leadership skill and **I is for Interviewing** because in the long and complex process of making good appointments the interview itself is the most significant component, but often the least satisfactory.

New staff are especially welcome, but the opportunity to appoint them rarely comes when and where you want it. The existing staff represents the school's most precious resource and **H is for Human resources** because a human resources (HR) specialist who looks after them–their appointment, professional development, promotion and succession–is an essential investment. The sum total of undergraduate and postgraduate education, pre-service and in-service training for a school's staff (and here I mean the whole staff) is formidable. A good HR department will help the leader unlock and develop that resource.

U is for Unacceptable performance, which happens in schools just as often as it does in other human organizations. Staff may be ill, burned out or worried about a domestic crisis; a few are no longer competent, some have lost all motivation and others are just plain lazy. Whatever the reason, their performance is not acceptable, and dealing with that in a firm, humane and consistent manner will quickly set a tone for human relationships within the schools. Most external advice will refer unhelpfully to "dead wood" and propose remedies that contradict every one of the school's much vaunted values.

Making it happen

There is little purpose in knowing what to do (which is often rather easy) unless you know how you are going to do it (which is usually rather difficult). The "what?" and the "how?" must go hand in hand, each shaping the other in a process that has been described, in the context of politics, as the "art of the possible". Nothing is more damaging to staff morale than a series of abandoned initiatives; nothing is more satisfying than a series of describable achievements–new buildings, curriculum reform, revised procedures, improved administrative structures, better student behaviour– that have been carefully planned and well executed.

So **M is for Making things happen**, and leaders must be ever conscious of the parameters within which they are operating; unfortunately, the sky is not the limit. Several of these shaping factors have already been introduced: playing by the rules, being sensitive to the local and national environment, working closely with the board, knowing one's own strengths and weaknesses and, above all, making the most of the school's human resource, its staff.

"Making the most of" is a laudable sentiment, but of little practical help. What does it mean in practice? Well, **J is for Job descriptions,** which does not sound particularly inspiring or visionary but represents that important bridge between a resource—in this case, the staff—and the capacity of someone to manage it. What are all those individuals contracted to do? Are they being appropriately rewarded? What skills do we have in abundance and where are the crucial skill gaps? At this point we are moving into the overlap between leadership and management—the latter best defined as achieving objectives on time and on budget—and the leader has a clear responsibility to create situations that are capable of being managed.

"On time and on budget". That reminds us of another important variable in the complex equation that relates vision to achievable reality. **F is for Finance** because money provides a powerful lever in determining what can and cannot be achieved. However enlightened the school's policies, however inspiring its values, however dedicated its staff, if the money has run out there will soon be no students left to inspire. As schools become more ambitious and more competitive, the search is on to find alternative sources of funding, and school heads can quickly find themselves devoting significant amounts of their time to fundraising.

An essential skill of leadership, one that is rarely acknowledged formally, is the ability to cut corners. Perhaps "set priorities" is more politically correct, but in the end it comes to the same thing. However well you manage your time, lean on your deputy's shoulder and delegate huge tasks to your colleagues, there are never enough hours in the day to read every important document in detail, to attend every important meeting, to talk to every important person and to write every important memo. Some things simply do not get done; the skill lies in making sure that the right things do not get done. In this way you can ensure that **N is for Nimbleness** and prevent the organization becoming bogged down in stifling bureaucracy.

Setting priorities and making choices, particularly the choice of doing nothing, involves a risk. Indeed, any change in direction involves a risk, and the leader who is not prepared to take one should remain tucked up in bed in the morning. Risks are to be welcomed, not feared, because making anything significant happen is a risk-taking process. So, **R is for Risk management,** which allows us to deal responsibly with risk—measuring, predicting and containing it so that it becomes friend rather than foe.

Many years ago I took the biggest professional risk of my career when I resigned from a tenured academic post in a lively department at a very well-regarded university. I had been appointed deputy head in a large comprehensive secondary school and it was to be my first experience of school leadership.

Some of the sections that follow are written to be inspirational in character while others are necessarily more mundane. Some take a helicopter perspective while others are rooted in the nuts and bolts of everyday experience. I believe that this mixture accurately reflects the reality of school leadership: a combination of vision and attention to the detail that allows that vision to be made real.

Much of my work has been in English state schools, but my more recent experience of different types of schools all around the world strongly encourages me to believe that my alphabetic choice will make widespread sense even in countries that do not use the alphabet. Some of the technical terms will differ but the same principles will apply whether the schools are large or small, secular or faith, selective or comprehensive, elementary, middle or high.

I have provided a brief glossary at the end of this book to explain some of the educational terminology that might be more peculiar to the British system. Leaders of schools bear many different titles: headmaster, headmistress, head teacher, principal, director, even director general. I have chosen to use the generic term "head".

Five different institutions play a part in this story, and each deserves a brief word of description.

Carisbrooke High School, where I was deputy head, was a senior high school of some 1,500 all-ability students aged 13–18 on the Isle of Wight. It had been created a year before my arrival by amalgamating two adjacent schools, one a grammar school and the other a secondary modern. It was one of four senior high schools on the island and its catchment area included the main town, Newport, and most of the rural area to the west. The head was Peter Cornall.

The Heathcote School, where I held my first headship, had opened as a secondary modern school in Stevenage. This was one of the so-called "new towns" that were built in the United Kingdom to relieve the acute shortage of housing in London following the devastation of the second world war. When I arrived, the school was educating about 850 students of all abilities, aged 11–18.

The Cavendish School, my second headship, was also located in a UK "new town", Hemel Hempstead, and came within the administration of the same local education authority as The Heathcote School (Hertfordshire County Council). It had opened as a selective grammar school and had acquired a reputation for being different, with an unusual curriculum and a young, lively faculty. During my headship The Cavendish School amalgamated with a nearby school to increase its size to about 1,300 all-ability students, aged 11–18.

The International School of Geneva, the world's oldest and largest international school, was founded in 1924 for the children of the employees of the League of Nations. By the time I arrived in 1991 as director general, it had grown to more than 3,000 students of 120 different nationalities, aged 4–19. Situated on three different campuses in and around Geneva, The International School of Geneva offered programmes in English, French and a mixture of the two.

The International Baccalaureate, of which I was appointed director general in 1999, is not so much a school as a family of schools—currently some 2,000, located in more than 120 different countries. It offers three challenging educational programmes for a worldwide community of schools, including the prestigious pre-university IB Diploma Programme. The International Baccalaureate is a truly global organization with principal offices in Buenos Aires, Cardiff, Geneva, New York and Singapore.

A is for Appraisal

How are we doing and how could we do better? Those two questions lie at the heart of appraisal—the formal process of evaluating the individual and the organization. So this is a good topic to introduce the challenge of leadership because effective systems of appraisal bring transparency, a culture of improvement and a structure of professional support. Bad systems breed suspicion and poor morale.

I remember the United Nations representative on the International School of Geneva's board of governors teasing me, "If you can introduce an effective system of staff appraisal we'll put up your statue." I did indeed introduce a system of staff appraisal, but two years after my departure it had vanished without trace and the statue was never erected. What went wrong? It was certainly not the careful preparation, which lasted a year and involved thorough training of appraisers and appraisees by an experienced consultant. It also involved seemingly endless dialogue with the teachers' unions representatives, who were deeply suspicious of the whole enterprise.

The teachers were won round but it was the sheer complexity of the procedures that destroyed it: too many forms to fill in and too many meetings to organize. Once the novelty wore off, the cumbersome process was squeezed out of busy schedules by more pressing priorities.

My advice for developing a system of appraisal would be to:

- keep it simple
- make it annual
- limit the answer boxes to a couple of A4 sides and,
- above all, maintain a sense of formality.

One essential purpose of appraisal is to provide a professional context that permits frank discussion of issues that would be embarrassingly out of place over coffee in the staff room. Never believe the head of department who claims to learn everything that needs to be known about colleagues over a drink after work.

Appraisal is often seen as a threat to the employee, but I regard it as an entitlement. Everyone has the professional right to a carefully prepared annual meeting with a line manager to discuss what has been achieved over the past year and what has led to frustration and failure. It is the moment to review last year's personal objectives, to relate them to the organization's overall goals and to retune them for the year ahead (in my experience objectives never fit neatly into a period of 12 months). It is also the moment to check the accuracy of the current job description and to ask what development support is appropriate and how it is best achieved within tight budgets. The answer sometimes lies in part-time doctorates, masters of business administration (MBAs) and winter seminars in tropical climes, but more often it can be found in the internal resource of the organization itself. A good school will have a mentoring system in place so that its huge accumulated corporate experience can be shared and tired teachers can be rejuvenated with a stimulating new responsibility.

Understandably, teachers want to know how the appraisal evidence is going to be used. As well as providing personal feedback and shaping professional development, will it be used in disciplinary action or, where appropriate, in contractual renewal or performance-related pay? The inevitable answer is: yes to all of them. While I cannot conceive of a teacher being dismissed on the sole evidence of an annual appraisal, I find it impossible to imagine a sensible disciplinary process that ignores it. It is in every employee's interest to have a written record of annual appraisal on file. Hopefully, this will have been agreed between appraiser and appraisee, but, if not, differences of opinion will have been recorded and serious disagreements resolved through an appeals procedure.

At the International Baccalaureate I appraised the seven directors who reported to me, but I also had a "grandfather role" for those who, in turn, reported to the directors. That meant reading and signing the appraisal reports of about another 50 staff at the level below director. This was very time-consuming but worth every minute because it was an effective way of feeling the pulse of the organization and keeping an eye both on future stars and on potential problems.

At The International School of Geneva I worked with an experienced consultant, who was a member of the governing board, to modify a "360-degree" appraisal instrument that she had designed for senior officials in the United Nations in Geneva and New York. Here was one of many examples of the value of the expertise that is present within most boards of governors. Four groups of people—the governing board, the senior management team, a sample of parents and a sample of teachers—were each asked to complete a questionnaire containing some 60 items about my leadership skills. These were divided into seven categories of leadership: organizational, financial, strategic, moral and so on.

The results were summarized and analysed by category of leadership skill and respondent and then reported to the board of governors. The subsequent discussion was always tough and often uncomfortable with an inevitable and understandable emphasis on Item 3, *Converts vision into action: makes things happen*, but the whole exercise was an indispensable part of my professional development, an example to the rest of the school and a key factor in my relationship with the board of governors. Whatever the discomfort, I was always encouraged to think that the Secretary General of the United Nations and his senior team were using a similar instrument, and when I moved to the International Baccalaureate the items were modified but the basic structure and process remained unchanged.

The organization itself, as well as the individuals who work within it, also needs to undergo regular appraisal. Most schools will be part of a local or a national scheme of inspection; some organizations will insist on authorizing their schools against published criteria; many independent schools will be accredited by an agency that offers a recognized and respected seal of approval.

Whatever the system and whatever its title, three factors are essential to a well-structured process of institutional appraisal.

- **What kind of school are you striving to be?** Whether a faith school, a specialist school, an all-ability school, a community college, whatever, an honest answer to this question is essential. The school's mission statement therefore spells out the true context of the appraisal because it says "this is what we are seeking to achieve".

- **The process of self-appraisal** ensures that the school itself retains the initiative, not some external body. This needs careful structuring, but the whole-hearted participation of the school community in evaluating its achievements and weaknesses is a crucial factor in determining the outcome, particularly in following up the inevitable recommendations for improvements.
- **Peer review** is arguably the most important factor. This is usually in the form of a visiting team who will read the account of the self-appraisal, spend several days in the school and reach its own conclusions, expressed in a written report of commendations and recommendations.

One particularly effective version of this process has been offered for many years by the Council of International Schools (CIS), and CIS accreditation is a much sought-after global recognition. I served my apprenticeship with CIS as a member of the visiting team for the United Nations International School in New York, where I first met the chairman of its board of governors, Kofi Annan. Two years later, I chaired a visiting team of 25 people for the accreditation of International College, Beirut, a distinguished trilingual (Arabic, English and French) school of 3,000 students situated on two separate campuses. From time to time I meet those team members and we still talk about that week as one of the most stimulating of our professional careers. Effective appraisal can therefore be a positive learning experience for everyone involved.

B

is for the Board

What do the following have in common? Colonel James Eldridge, Councillor Brian Hall, Councillor Mavis Stannard, the Reverend Alfred Speed, Arthur Jennings, Asha Singh-Willams, Ambi Sundaram, the Honourable Greg Crafter and Dr Monique Seefried. To judge from their names and titles, not a lot, but they were the nine chairs of the five different boards of governors I have worked with. The fact that I can still remember all their names is a sign of the close and special relationship that often exists between the head and the chair of governors. Of course, they all had something else in common: they were passionately concerned to see their institution enjoy success and win respect in the community, even though I have to admit that they often went about it in rather different ways.

School boards come in all shapes and sizes and with several different titles. They may be known as governing boards, or boards of trustees, or (in the United States) boards of education, and the range of their responsibilities will vary depending upon the system (public, private, faith, international) and the country. In American public schools the strong influence of the district superintendent provides a professional buffer between the board of education and the group of schools it serves. By contrast, in the UK each school has its own board of governors that has considerable autonomy in its responsibility for the school. There are, of course, schools that do not have a board, but I find it hard to understand how these work. The board speaks on behalf of the school's community, determines the school's strategy and provides a last court of appeal. I cannot believe that any single individual, particularly the owner of the school, can ever do that.

Let me start at Carisbrooke High School, where I was the deputy head. The head, Peter Cornall, insisted that I attend all the meetings of the board of governors and, where appropriate, make a full contribution to the proceedings. This was just one example of his thoughtful mentoring in the art of leadership. So, when a few years later I attended my first board meeting as a head, there were few surprises. I had learned not only to take the governors seriously, but to help them carry out their difficult task effectively and I have often asked the simple question, "is the board of governors respected by the staff of the school?" That, for me, is the touchstone of success, and if the answer is "no" then I must take some of the blame.

> It was at The Cavendish School that I came to recognize the importance of a board of governors that was truly representative of the school's stakeholders. We were scheduled to merge with a rather unpopular neighbouring school whose prospects had been fatally damaged by falling student numbers. The move was certain to be resisted by many parents, who feared the effects of a five-year upheaval of new buildings, split-site working and unfamiliar teachers on the education of their children. However, the board of governors was totally committed to the change and backed it, and me, through thick and thin. The chair, who had been a founder governor of the school, had the good sense to stand down—his hearing was no longer sharp enough to allow him to control the increasingly lively meetings—and the board wisely replaced him with the chair of the other school's governors. His wisdom and leadership had a decisive influence on the success of the merger.

One cannot overvalue the key relationship that exists in many school systems between the head and the chair of the board of governors. It must be close but never cosy, based upon a mutual respect that is best developed in the context of a strategic plan and a set of annual objectives derived from that plan. In the schools in which I have worked the board appointed the head, appraised the head and, as a last resort, dismissed the head. These two people must decide how to achieve a balance between what busy governors need to know and a realistic assessment of the time they have to absorb it, and that depends upon effective communication. That requires:

- face-to-face meetings
- regular written reports
- telephone conferences and
- an interactive Internet site.

I also found an annual off-site workshop involving board members and senior faculty very helpful as a way of getting to know each other and to understand better the circumstances under which each group operated.

At The International School of Geneva I inherited a board of governors that was and remained, despite my best efforts, dysfunctional. The membership was overloaded with parents and former students, a lethal combination. The former wanted action by the end of the week, usually on some trivial issue that directly affected their own children, while the latter wanted to preserve the traditions of their own golden age a generation earlier. There was no sense of corporate responsibility, and bad-tempered meetings would end well after midnight.

My life was made tolerable only by the dedication and unwavering support of two outstanding chairs, both senior executives with the World Health Organization. Even so, I needed all my political skills, by then well tested over many years of school leadership, to enable me to steer the school between the obstacles littered by different board members. Their turnover was so great that by the time I left the school not a single member responsible for my appointment eight years earlier remained. I had outlived them all and could begin to see them in a different and less threatening perspective. But this is not the way I like to work, and perhaps the biggest pleasure in moving to the International Baccalaureate was to find a board whose members generally had no personal stake in the organization and could therefore take a detached, long-term view of its needs.

Handbooks on the subject of governance, and there are plenty of them, will tell you to maintain a clear dividing line between governance and management, but the reality is rather different. The head of a school will want to influence long-term strategy and a wise board will take the head's advice seriously. At the same time, the board will have sensible views, usually based on substantial and varied experience, on how the organization should be managed. No matter how clearly the tasks and responsibilities of both parties are described, there will remain an ill-defined area that is the legitimate territory of both governance and management. Negotiations within this area will help to define the well-being of the organization as well as the longevity of the head.

In the UK, it was taken for granted that the students' voice would be heard at meetings of the board of governors even though their representatives might, for legal reasons, be unable to vote. I insisted on two student representatives (one would have found the formality rather daunting) and I would invite them to coffee beforehand to analyse the meeting's agenda and anticipate particular items to which they would probably be invited to contribute. I also encouraged the chair to make sure that the students were fully involved and, as a result, their contributions were invariably helpful and taken seriously. Without doubt the presence of students on a governing board encourages good behaviour and also ensures that meetings come to an end before the early hours of the morning.

C is for Change

No brook is here; I feel the loss,
From home and friends and all alone.

So wrote the English poet John Clare in 1832 after moving from the village of Helpstone, where he had lived all his life, to nearby Northborough. The two villages were only three miles apart but the change was completely destabilizing. Clare could no longer locate the familiar sights and sounds that had given him his daily bearings, and he spent much of the rest of his life confined to an asylum. This is an extreme example of the disorientation, perhaps bereavement is not too strong a term, that can be caused by unfamiliar events and surroundings. As leadership is frequently defined as "the capacity to bring about change", wise leaders will think hard about the possible consequences of their actions. The adrenaline that stimulates the mental reflexes of the leader will often knot the stomachs of those who are being led.

If an organization is to prosper in the long term it must be ready to adapt to the new challenges of its changing environment. Nonetheless, the question should always be asked whether the change under discussion is in the best interests of the organization or merely in the personal interests of those proposing it. "If it ain't broke, why fix it?" is an uncomfortable question that always deserves a compelling answer.

At The Heathcote School, very little seemed to need fixing. The school was popular with parents; the faculty was a good mix of youth and experience; morale seemed to be generally high. But I felt the school was trapped in its secondary modern origins and part of the problem was the way the curriculum was made available to students. Each new intake of about 150 students was divided into two bands on the basis of … quite frankly, I have forgotten on what basis. Was it the recommendations from their primary schools? Was it tests that we set in the first week of term? Whatever it was, it seemed to me to be unreliable, but it had important consequences because a different curriculum was then provided for each band. Immediately, students were divided, some labelled as "academic", the rest as "non-academic", and, predictably enough, they soon behaved according to those labels.

All this made nonsense of the school's claim to be "comprehensive". What we needed was a more flexible system that maintained a common curriculum, ideally during the compulsory years of education to age 16. At the same time it needed to recognize wide differences in ability, background and learning styles, particularly in linear subjects, such as modern languages and mathematics, and to allow an appropriate response to the special educational needs of many students. The answer lay in the technique known as "block timetabling", and it needed someone who understood how it worked. At this point I am reminded of the comment made by the legendary chief executive officer of General Electric, Jack Welch, who said that strategic planning will come to nothing unless you have the right people in the right place at the right time.

The right person was our senior teacher. He understood the timetable and he had immediate sympathy with my aims—I suspect he was a late developer himself; he had an Open University (OU) degree and was now a tutor for the OU. The technical puzzle clearly appealed to his chess-playing nature. Even so, the proposed change needed some careful selling: it would present a particular challenge to certain teachers who had traditionally worked only with the academic band of students; it would produce some winners (the creative arts would attract more able students) and some losers (history and geography lost some periods). But overall it had a compelling simplicity and it gave welcome autonomy to heads of departments to organize their students into the teaching groups that best suited their subject.

This provides a good example of what I have described as a "reversible change", borrowing the phrase from physics. In thermodynamics a reversible change takes place when the system that is changing remains in equilibrium with its surroundings. In practice, this is never completely achievable, but a battery offers an example of a chemical change that is close to being reversible, and we should note that it produces useful work in the form of electricity. The change described above was literally reversible in the sense that, had it failed, we could have returned without much damage to the same state as before, but in addition it was relatively unthreatening:

- it built upon existing experience (English and mathematics were already blocked on the timetable)
- it was wholly consistent with the relatively new comprehensive status of the school
- I like to think that it encouraged the production of useful energy, just like a battery.

A rather different problem confronted me in Geneva. When I arrived in 1991 the school was close to civil war, and the board, far from offering a solution, was clearly a large part of the problem. It was soon clear that in the short term I would never reform the board, and indeed all my suggestions concerning its size, composition and terms of reference fell on deaf ears. How could I moderate its influence in a way that would also anticipate the likely future development of the school?

The answer was to look more carefully at the structure of this huge school, which was located on three separate campuses, each too distant from the others to allow any day-to-day interaction or cooperation. For all practical purposes—a reality that the board seemed unwilling to recognize—each campus was an autonomous organization with its own staff and buildings, its own community and its own distinctive culture. I strongly believe that an effective school builds a strong relationship with its own community, and that would happen only if each campus had its own mini-board, which I called a campus development group (CDG). Unlike the board, they would have true stakeholder representation, including faculty members and students. Unlike the board, they would discuss only issues of immediate relevance to the campus. Unlike the board, their meetings would close before the early hours of the morning.

However, there was a catch to all this because only the board itself could authorize the new CDGs. In the end it responded to mounting community pressure by approving a pilot project. Now the pilot project has an important role to play in the process of change. If the change is successful, then the pilot can expand smoothly into a full-blown operation; if not, it can be quietly buried without anyone losing face. In the event, the CDGs proved successful and today they are ready for the moment when the Foundation (currently numbering more than 3,500 students) reaches a critical mass and divides painlessly into its largely autonomous constituent campuses.

Here, then, was a change that, while worthwhile in itself, contained the seeds of a bigger change to come. It illustrates a simple formula that has helped me to think about change. It is known as Gleicher's formula and it says that the change will take place successfully only if:

$$D \times V \times F > C$$

- *D* is dissatisfaction with the status quo.
- *V* is a clear vision of something better.
- *F* is knowledge of the first steps to be taken.

The combination of these factors must exceed *C*, the cost of the change (financial and psychological). The formula reminds us that many changes fail through a lack of an understanding of the first practical steps. The starting point is obvious—where we are now. The finishing post is usually clearly described—where we want to get to. It is planning the steps in between, and especially that crucial first move, that will determine the ultimate success.

D is for Delegation

Delegation means asking someone else to do something on your behalf. It also means giving your colleague the resource and the authority to do it successfully. Successful leaders are usually rather good at delegation because of a simple effect of natural selection. If you cannot delegate you accumulate too many tasks and the resulting stress eventually kills you.

Of course, you can never delegate the responsibility for the final outcome. A thread will always connect you to the delegated issue, and knowing how best to manage that thread is the key to effective delegation.

The thread should never be drawn too tight. Delegating responsibility is not asking someone else to present your solution in different wrapping paper. It will be their solution, not yours, and it may be one that you do not wholly agree with. There is a puzzling convention in some schools that all letters should be signed by the head, irrespective of who actually wrote them. This is surely an example of drawing the thread too tight to the point of disempowering one's colleagues.

The thread should never be broken. Having delegated a task, it is essential not to interfere even when things appear to be going wrong. The colleague must be given time and space to sort it out, and some of my biggest mistakes have come from impatient interference.

One winter's evening, a car was driving slowly out of the school gates when it was hit by an ambush of snowballs. As luck would have it, the driver was a governor and she was not amused. Nor was I amused when the wheels of enquiry into the incident seemed to grind slowly and ineffectively. My reputation as guardian of a well-disciplined school was on the line so I decided to intervene from on high. My investigation was a total disaster, not only failing to identify the culprits, but alienating those who had been working conscientiously to do just that. It also made me look rather foolish.

The understandable urge "to show them how to do it" should always be curbed because it is the very denial of delegation. I was once so unhappy with the performance of some of the class tutors that I decided to become one myself the following school year, despite my huge responsibilities as a deputy head, in order to set an example. Fortunately for my reputation, a very senior member of staff fell ill during the summer holidays and my irresponsible ambition was quickly lost in the resulting crisis of redistributing responsibilities.

The thread must be wide enough to encourage communication at an appropriate level of understanding. This will mean arranging discussions on a regular basis rather than hastily convening a meeting when a crisis seems to be looming.

As a deputy head I used to make the school's timetable, but when I became a head I delegated this vital task to a senior colleague. Nothing would frustrate me more than a last-minute plea, "I am having a real problem fitting in 4Y's German next year; can you sort it out for me?" I was in no position to sort it out, lacking the necessary detailed background knowledge—the very reason for delegating the task in the first place. In order to be of any help, I needed information at a much higher level. For example, I could readily respond to the statement, "I have two alternatives for 4Y's German next year. The first will give Frau Schmidt a miserable timetable and she may resign. The second will mean teaching them a double period on a Friday afternoon. Which do you prefer?"

The thread of delegation must ensure that an issue is addressed at the point at which it is most clearly perceived and understood. However, this can sometimes be a tough process involving considerable trust and therefore considerable risk.

A young student of 15 was taken into care because of physical abuse by her parents. It was a very serious case involving the police and the social and medical services. A case conference was called to bring all the players together to decide what to do and I was invited to participate with other senior officials. I decided not to go and instead passed the invitation on to the student's tutor, who knew her the best. I can imagine that some eyebrows were raised when a young and relatively inexperienced teacher sat down amidst all the top brass, but I trusted her not only to make an appropriate contribution to the conference but also to be an effective ambassador for the school. Subsequent feedback confirmed that I was right on both counts.

The thread of delegation brings important professional development opportunities. The young teacher who walked into the case conference mentioned above was a different person to the young teacher who walked out. The experience of successful delegation will often be the key to promotion because a hugely important factor at interview is the ability to say, "Yes, I have done that. I know just what it feels like."

How many times has my heart sunk when a much-valued colleague has come back from interview to announce a deserved promotion? I hope my external smile and words of congratulation have concealed my inner turmoil. There is some consolation in the knowledge that the world's graveyards are full of indispensable people and, tough though it is at the time, it should surely be every leader's ambition to see colleagues move on and up. The average age of the faculty at The Cavendish School was close to 30, and the staff room was full of young, talented and ambitious teachers. Every year a handful moved on to posts of greater seniority and today, as they approach the end of their careers, many of them occupy positions of significant responsibility in the world of education. I am very proud of that.

The thread of delegation often leads to the school's deputy heads. I have been unusually fortunate in my deputies, starting with my first headship, when they must have wondered what was in store for them with the arrival of a young and inexperienced new boss. The young and inexperienced new boss wondered what was in store for him, working with deputies old enough to be his parents who had been part of the school since its opening. None of us need have worried, but I have no doubt who learned the most from the relationship. Deputies will have their own specific tasks—the curriculum, staff development, buildings, community relations, whatever—but their first responsibility is to deputize for the head, and they should be given ample opportunity to do that. They also have a responsibility to keep the head alert.

- Did you read this article in last week's local paper?
- Did you see that programme on television last night?
- Did you notice there is an interesting conference coming up next month?
- Do you want to borrow this library book?

are all questions I have heard, appreciated, encouraged and come to expect from my deputies. They also have a responsibility to provide broad shoulders to cry on. Small wonder, then, that I have remained in touch with my deputies, who contributed so much to the development of my own career.

E is for Environmental awareness

In 1985 I spent a term's secondment with the multinational chemical company, ICI. It was the start of a stimulating relationship that culminated in my appointment a few years later as the company's education consultant. I had studied chemistry at university so I was fascinated to observe real chemistry carried out on a huge scale. As an educator I came to understand better the connection between the quality of state education and the creation of wealth. The report that I wrote of my experience was entitled "Isn't that rather commercial?"–a provocative reference to the comment of a colleague who believed my secondment would unwisely blur a necessary distinction between education and business and that I was supping with the devil.

How the educational environment has changed since then! Today no one questions the relationship between a nation's capacity to create wealth and its ability to afford high-quality education. No one questions the reverse process either, namely the investment in high-quality education that brings improved economic performance. The two have not just become blurred; they are seen as intertwined. The 1980s were a time of exciting change when effective schools were no longer content to be isolated islands of intellectual enlightenment in a sea of industrial ignorance but aimed to be an integral, influential part of the surrounding environment.

The "surrounding environment" has two different but related meanings: the immediate community of the school with which it interacts on a daily basis and the national social, economic and political scene that influences its long-term future. The astute leader keeps closely in touch with both.

The Heathcote School had very close relationships with the major employer in Stevenage: British Aerospace, or BAe as it was trendily rebranded. Many of our parents worked for BAe, and many of their children were destined to join them. The head of the apprentice school was a good friend of the school and a regular visitor. It was he who arranged for me to spend a week of the summer holidays working in the company, and that experience left me with one overwhelming impression: the growing importance of computers. It was evident even then (this was 1978) that computers were going to transform not just the way we worked but the way we lived our lives and interacted with other people's lives. A few years later I persuaded Rank-Xerox to give The Cavendish School a word processor for the school office and the information communication technology (ICT) revolution had begun.

The above story also illustrates, sadly, the danger of being too far ahead of the game. A few years after the generosity of Rank-Xerox had transformed the administration of our office, the local education authority started to implement its own policy of ICT in schools. Needless to say, it was based upon completely different hardware, software and protocols and we were left isolated, far behind the pack. I was reminded of this when a similar situation arose many years later when the International Baccalaureate made itself a pioneer in the field of on-screen marking of examination scripts. Alas, we lacked the resource to develop our initiative and instead we were gradually overhauled by a major publisher who was able make the necessary substantial investment. Being aware of the environment does not necessarily mean being ahead of it unless you have the means to capitalize on that early advantage.

Religion is often an important part of the school's environment, and representatives of the different denominations were always regular visitors to Carisbrooke High School. Alas, relationships with one vicar were not good. I could understand his disapproval of students leaving discarded fish and chip wrappings in the graveyard, but he seemed much more interested in the physical condition of his church than the spiritual condition of the souls who might use it, especially young and troubled souls. We never won the war but we scored an important temporary victory when he relented one year and allowed us to hold a Christmas carol service in his beautiful Norman building.

This was an early move in a much wider strategy to meet the community on its own ground. Carisbrooke High School served the town of Newport and the western half of the Isle of Wight, a vast rural catchment area, and the remoteness of many parents prevented them from attending evening parents' meetings in the school. In any case, some of them found an invitation to the school, which seemed so distant from their daily lives, a daunting prospect. So we brought the meetings to them, taking over a pub or village hall and introducing the evening with music or a small drama presentation. The school also became an agent for the arts, organizing visits to concert halls and opera houses on the mainland, often chartering a hovercraft to deliver us back to the island late at night. Thus, the conventional model of the focused community school was effectively turned upside down.

The benefits of a supportive relationship between the school and the local community were brought home to me one day when I was telephoned by a reporter from the local newspaper. He told me that he was writing a feature based on a story from a parent who had complained that the school was completely neglecting her daughter's education. Would I like to respond to the complaint? I decided I would not, but instead checked the student's background and rang the paper's editor. I told him that the accusation was false and could do serious, mischievous harm to the school's reputation. The editor said he had no means of judging between me and the parent so I suggested he spend the next 24 hours contacting a sample of parents in order to assess more accurately the school's local reputation. He rang back a day later to say the article would not be printed and I gave silent thanks for a supportive community.

I have made a distinction between the school's awareness of its local and national environment. But, increasingly, the awareness must be global, and for an international school the catchment area is indeed the world itself. The International School of Geneva, for example, educated students of 120 different nationalities, speaking more than 80 different mother tongues. The only meaningful concept of an environment was the whole planet, and if this sounds fanciful then international educators would insist that it defines their challenge, namely to educate future citizens of the world. In this task, the school in Geneva drew inspiration from the League of Nations, which had assisted its foundation in 1924, and from the United Nations, which was formally represented on its board of governors. The school's charter speaks of "the preparation of students for reintegration into their own cultures or for integration into other cultures", which opens up a whole new perspective on the concept of the environment and the purpose of education.

In an international school one cannot afford to neglect relationships with the host country. Once, in Switzerland, I was formally summoned by the *préfet* (state representative) in Nyon to explain why the school had failed to observe the strict cantonal work permit regulations in making a faculty appointment.

"I'm sure I've seen you somewhere before," he said as I entered his office.

"Yes," I replied, "We invited you to the opening of our new laboratories last month."

"Oh, yes, that was a wonderful lunch. Well I don't expect you've done anything too awful."

I escaped with *une amende symbolique*, a trivial symbolic fine.

F

is for Finance

Mission and vision are inspiring concepts, but they look a little forlorn when the cash runs out. A prudent leader keeps a very close eye on the bottom line of the balance sheet. Heads of schools are rarely sacked for professional incompetence, moral turpitude or even raving insanity; the official reason is always financial mismanagement. So a phone call a day to your financial manager will keep all kinds of nasty consequences at bay. But that assumes that you can trust your financial manager to give you accurate, honest information. I judged them on their capacity to deliver bad news in a way that made me listen to it calmly and dispassionately. "Enrolment is below prediction, Customs and Excise has changed its mind about a tax rebate, the dollar has weakened still further, all of which knocks around a quarter of a million off the bottom line." Then, while half of me is desperately wondering what size of hole this will make in the budget, the other half is saying thank-you for this prompt and accurate information. Because if you appear to resent bad news, and if you punish the messenger who brings it, then bad news will be concealed and before long you will be in terminally deep trouble.

There is an important difference between taking an intelligent interest and interfering in an activity that you have delegated to someone else who is better qualified to deal with it. Part of the answer lies in the information that you seek and the way that you look for it, both elements of that essential "thread of delegation". Some of your questions will be probing:

- Shouldn't the figure at the bottom of Table 3 be the same as the figure at the top of Table 5?

while others will be seeking clarification:

- Can you explain—once again, I'm afraid!—what is meant by 'deferred income'?

Often you will be seeking trends:

- What did this figure look like at the same time last year?

or making an assessment of risk:

- What is the worst-case scenario if we don't increase fees by cost of living next year?

But there is much more to it than taking an intelligent interest, because the leader must be able to make an accurate assessment of the organization's financial health. So another part of the answer lies in following key performance indicators which assess different parts of the organization's financial health, rather like measuring a patient's blood pressure, temperature, cholesterol level and so on. These will include:

- income
- cash balance
- debtors
- staff costs relative to income
- reserves.

The important point is not the figure itself, but its comparison with the targets that have been set as part of the budget. Only then will warning lights flash in time for corrective measures to be taken. But the head must be able to interpret the evidence, and I feel genuinely anxious for those who cannot juggle figures with confidence, make approximations, check a column total for the right order of magnitude, extrapolate from this year to the next, quickly interpret the axes of a graph and move from fractions to percentages and back again. I have no simple answer: the innumerate head is a vulnerable head.

With each successive school, I have become more deeply involved in financial management, in line with the increasing autonomy of each institution. Carisbrooke High School answered entirely to the local education authority. Each year a nominal sum was allocated depending upon the number of students and their ages (it was known as "capitation") and we were merely responsible for dividing it between the different spending departments–science, humanities, the library, guidance and so on. All orders were placed with a buyer called County Supplies, which purchased in bulk for the local education authority, and no real money was exchanged. At The Heathcote School, we actually had the money in a bank account so it was possible to take advantage of bargain offers, and for the first time an element of competition was introduced and a new word started to enter the vocabulary–"virement"–meaning that the school could transfer money allocated for one purpose in order to use it for another, though not at this stage for extra staffing. The Cavendish School saw the dawn of a new era known as LMS–the local management of schools–which meant that the board of governors was held fully accountable for the budget.

The arrival of LMS signalled the inevitable decline of the local authority's own advisory services. Schools were now free to purchase their own advice, and consultants of dubious provenance and even more dubious quality popped up like mushrooms. As a head in one of the most widely respected local education authorities, I had been able to pick up the telephone and speak to an expert on almost any issue from the design of laboratories to nutritious meals, from computerized library software to children with impaired hearing. That was changing, but by now I had moved to Geneva, where I would be responsible for every aspect of the school's finances described in a very large annual budget.

The annual budget lies at the heart of an organization. That is an entirely apt metaphor; the budget drives resources around the organization in a manner that controls the functioning of its different constituent parts. Alas, too many people see it as a daunting list of figures that, at some point, somewhere on the page, should add up to zero. It is a sinister aide-memoire, a statement of the amount available to spend during the year and a constant, threatening reminder that it is nowhere near enough.

In fact, with the possible exception of the strategic plan, the school's budget is its most important document. Indeed, it is an integral part of the strategic plan, the annual exercise, never perfect and always a compromise, to turn the strategic plan into the day-to-day reality of what the organization can actually do, what it can really achieve. The budget is therefore not a list of figures, it is a story that explains how progress will be achieved. Each year the head should be challenged to tell that story to the board of governors, to explain just how the budget has been constructed to take forward the aims of the strategic plan. All too often the board is either satisfied to see a bottom-line surplus without asking what any of the intervening lines means or is confused by the nit-picking behaviour of those who can never see the overall wood for the columns of trees.

In an ideal world each new budget would start from scratch with a clean sheet of paper on which every single item of expenditure would be uniquely justified. The real world is not like that, partly through lack of time but chiefly because much of the year's expenditure becomes locked into the budget: it is the annual cost of "business as usual". In practice, zero-based budgeting happens just once, when the organization is created, but it is still worth trying to peel away the previous layers of accretion in order to expose some of the assumptions about "business as usual" that have built up, unchallenged, over the years.

Given that this year's budget will be the starting point for next year's budget, how should we proceed? More important: *who* should proceed? How widely should the process involve the staff and who will actually make the decisions? There is no simple answer to this (except, ultimately, the board must finally approve the budget) but my instinct is always to share knowledge, to share problems, to share possible solutions and thereby to increase the overall store of knowledge and the sense of corporate responsibility. These, after all, are the two essential components of empowerment: appropriate knowledge and a shared understanding of the parameters within which that knowledge can be deployed.

The head must always be at the centre of this process; it is not wise to risk being absent from meetings of finance committees. Then, when the budget is in operation, those questions to the financial manager and that interpretation of the key performance indicators can be based on an intimate knowledge of the budget's overall structure and purpose. If others feel more comfortable with the figures, the head can at least articulate the story of what the budget is designed to achieve.

G is for Generosity

My headmaster when I was a student at Watford Boys' Grammar School (WBGS) was a remarkable man called Harry Rée. Years later I worked in his department at the University of York and he became a lifelong mentor and friend. My thinking and my whole career owe much to his example and guidance. He once told me that when he was being interviewed for the headship of WBGS he was asked to describe the most important quality of a headmaster. "I had no idea what they were looking for," he recalled, "but quite suddenly, out of the blue, the answer came into my head. 'Generosity', I replied."

Sadly, generosity is often perceived as a weak virtue. Giving things away, particularly in tough negotiations, is seen either as short-term capitulation that inevitably leads to long-term trouble or as evidence of having too much in the first place. Generosity is associated with appeasement but, paradoxically, that is why I regard it as a tough virtue, precisely because it *is* open to abuse, it can be taken advantage of and thrown back in your face. The giver is taking a significant risk but in doing so recognizes the possibility that a difficult situation might be transformed, a deadlock broken or a conflict prevented.

In the sixth century BC, the Athenian statesman Solon revised the city-state's constitution. Amongst many other reforms, he cancelled all debts, freed all debt-slaves and banned the securing of loans against personal freedom. It became known as the *seisachtheia*—the shaking off of burdens. I first heard about this remarkable act of generosity in a memorable lecture given by Robert Birley, the distinguished former headmaster of Eton College, at the University of Cape Town, when I was studying there as a postgraduate student. Verwoerd was Prime Minister of South Africa, and the apartheid regime was at its most repressive. Birley was therefore taking a considerable risk by commending Solon's reforms to the all-white, minority government. He quoted the powerful fragment left by Democritus, writing a century after Solon, and almost certainly inspired by Solon's action:

> *When the powerful in a state, face to face with the weak, are prepared to make financial sacrifices for them and to help them and to satisfy them, that is the time when you get, first, compassion and then the end to isolation and the appearance of comradeship and mutual defence, and then civic agreement and then other benefits beyond the capacity of anyone to enumerate in full.*

I know of no better description of the power of generosity. Twenty-five years after I listened to Robert Birley, Nelson Mandela was released from prison on Robben Island and showed the same measure of generosity towards his former captors, oppressors and tormentors, uniquely establishing the pathway to the end of apartheid and the transfer to democratic government in South Africa.

In a school, generosity is most effectively displayed in the form of forgiveness of errors. I remember conducting an annual appraisal with a financial manager and telling him that my only criticism of his year's performance was that he did not seem to have made any mistakes. I suggested this meant either that he was concealing them or that he was unusually competent. In fact, it was much more of the latter than the former, but I wanted to emphasize the point that the longer he tried to maintain a clean sheet, the more difficult it would become to confess the inevitable mistake, and in financial matters that could have very serious consequences. Of course, as I have already conceded, some people will abuse the generosity of forgiveness and use it—abuse it—as a welcome safety net for their laziness or incompetence; they are not interested in learning from their mistakes. But in my experience this is rare and I would much rather encourage a forgiving than a punitive organizational culture.

Forgiving is not the same as forgetting, and turning a blind eye to mistakes helps no one. The key here is timing, choosing the appropriate moment and setting. This will depend to some extent on personal chemistry and the unplanned, informal, one-to-one contact may be just the right moment to bring up and resolve a past indiscretion. Personally, I prefer a measure of formality and expectation that need be no more threatening than a note saying "Can we find a moment before the end of this week to talk about ...?"

Sometimes the rewards of generosity can be out of all proportion to the size of the gesture. Each autumn, the personnel manager of the International Baccalaureate office in Geneva would come to discuss with me the discretionary holiday to be given between Christmas Day and New Year's Day. I invariably agreed a generous allocation, not to win the cheap approval of the staff, but to recognize that many of them were involved in extensive and exhausting travel throughout the rest of the year and here was a small, practical way for me to recognize it, particularly at a time of year when they could spend it quietly with their family and friends. Their gratitude was as great as the envy of the staff in our other offices, where I found it more difficult to interfere!

There is another way for a leader to show generosity which has a more subtle influence on the culture of an organization. As well as defining generosity as the desire to give good things to others, why not include managing without desirable things oneself? Sacrifice is much too strong a word, but a good leader will curb a desire to flaunt the trappings of authority. The choice of words, of a meeting venue, of office furniture, of a working language—these are examples of small opportunities to show generosity of spirit. I remember the words of my deputy in Geneva, who insisted: "Why exert your right to order a taxi when you are on a bus route?"

Finally, generosity provides an important antidote to an undesirable feature of many professional organizations, best described as *schadenfreude*, the pleasure taken from someone else's misfortunes. This is not wholly unexpected when most well-placed professionals are the successes of a highly competitive culture. I passed my examinations because others failed theirs; I went to university because others did not; I obtained my first job and my subsequent promotions by beating others. Professionals do not achieve success in their careers by saying "after you", and this can build a strongly negative culture, particularly when it rubs off from teacher to student. In fact, my own personal experience has been very different, and my first three jobs, which turned out to be crucial to the development of my subsequent career, were obtained because those making the appointments were willing to take an unusually generous view of my limited experience and not entirely relevant qualifications. Others must judge whether the gamble paid off, but I have never forgotten my debt of gratitude for their generosity.

H is for Human resources

I belong to that fortunate generation that paid no university tuition fees and even received a means-tested grant to meet my living expenses. I therefore had no financial debt hanging over me when I started teaching and I became so quickly absorbed in my work that each monthly pay cheque came as a surprise, an unexpected bonus. I had no idea who paid me or if the amount was correct and I can still remember my amazement when an older colleague banged his way into the staff room complaining furiously about a trivial error in his monthly salary, which was so much higher than mine. I was young, with few responsibilities, and my whole life revolved around the school that quickly became not only a place of work, but a social club for making friends and a focus for sport and music.

It was fun, but it was a woefully inadequate preparation for my later responsibilities. Someone should have explained to me the details of my contract, the way the school fitted into the local structure of state education and the nature of its funding. Someone should have told me about the role of the teachers' professional associations (I joined one reluctantly only to ensure legal protection). Someone should have been thinking about the development of my career and overseen the process of my annual appraisal. In other words, the school lacked a "someone" with overall responsibility for the school's human resources: their appointment, induction, development and eventual departure. As a young science teacher I had outstanding support from within my department but virtually none from elsewhere. No resource is more precious to a school than its staff, which typically will account for at least 75% of its annual expenditure.

When leaving the University of York to become deputy head at Carisbrooke High School, I went to say farewell to the vice-chancellor, Lord James. Before becoming the founding vice-chancellor at York, Eric James had been the distinguished high master of Manchester Grammar School in the north of England, and his parting advice to me was typically forthright and practical: "It's the teachers that make an effective school. Of course it's wonderful to have a large library, pleasant playing fields, modern laboratories and so on but in the end it is the teachers who count." And as I reached the door he shouted after me, "And never forget; while there's death there's hope!"

Perhaps it was this advice that encouraged me always to keep close to the school's staffing situation, to try to keep a finger on its pulse, either directly, through a deputy, or through someone specifically in charge of human resources. In doing so I have been encouraged to learn that successful industrial leaders such as Jack Welch and Bill Gates spent a disproportionate amount of their time involved in making key appointments, not only of their immediate colleagues but of a surprisingly wide pool of senior executives. Of all the qualities that I admire in leaders, the one I think most desirable is their capacity to make consistently high-quality staff appointments. The secret, I am convinced, is never to compromise, never to accept second best just because a vacancy must be filled as a deadline approaches. It is far better to wait, to make a temporary appointment, and then to try again to find someone of proven quality or (and this is much more difficult to judge) of real potential.

The "laissez-faire" approach of my early professional experience had many benefits. I worked long hours, many of them voluntarily, became involved in important curriculum developments, coached rugby and athletics and helped with all kinds of musical activities. School occupied my whole life, and it never really occurred to me that others might view it differently, that they might perceive teaching as a job rather than as a vocation.

My awakening came in the mid-1980s when frustration with pay and conditions of service provoked the UK teachers' professional associations into a national work-to-rule, recommending withdrawal from all voluntary activities. Now well into my second school headship, I was forced to weigh the teachers' ill-defined contractual duties against their moral responsibilities, which were even less clearly defined. It was an uncomfortable experience for everyone, but for me it brought a change of attitude. In future, I knew that I could no longer rely on "goodwill" that could be switched on and off depending upon the prevailing political and economic climate.

From that moment on I was determined to bring the greatest possible clarity to the rights and responsibilities of all members of staff from the time they applied for a post to the moment when they left the school. For example, there must be:

- clear, published policies for advertising vacant posts and interviewing candidates
- detailed job descriptions
- a programme of induction for all new members of staff, which might well involve an element of mentoring
- clear guidelines concerning the amount of money available for professional development and how it is accessed
- agreement on how the annual appraisal report can be used
- defined contractual obligations for attendance at staff meetings, staff training days and meetings with parents
- a description of the opportunities and entitlements for secondments, sabbatical leave and unpaid leave of absence
- agreed procedures for illness or other forms of incapacity.

These are just some of the situations that need describing and explaining, always recognizing that recourse to a formal process of appeal may be necessary if agreement cannot be reached. In many cases, of course, much of this will be at the discretion not of the school, but of the local education authority or board of education, but that makes it even more important that the information should be made available, ideally in a single handbook, to all members of staff.

Within the first year of my appointment at the International School of Geneva, I was involved in the complex negotiation of a so-called *convention collective*, which defined in great detail every aspect of the rights and responsibilities of the different categories of staff: faculty, administrative and technical. It was a huge undertaking, light years away from my early, informal and ill-defined British experience, but it was well worth every minute of the investment of time because it was the single most important factor in the process of bringing peace to a very troubled school. The agreement was renegotiated every five years with the salary scales that formed part of it being reviewed every three years, following a comparative analysis with a sample of other schools, national and international.

The tight definition of legal rights and responsibilities need not inhibit voluntary contributions; on the contrary, teachers with an unambiguous contract will feel less vulnerable to exploitation and therefore often more ready to contribute. The Geneva *convention collective* contained a phrase to the effect that contributions to extracurricular activities were encouraged and welcomed but did not form part of the teacher's formal contract. Everyone knew where they stood and there was a rich programme of voluntary activities.

I is for Interviewing

Arguably the most important component of selecting high quality staff is the interview, and research has shown that the right kind of interview can be a powerful instrument in making the right choice. It is a more reliable indicator of suitability than references or tests of ability or personality. However, the same research shows that the wrong kind of interview can be a very poor predictor so, bearing in mind the huge investment that a new member of staff represents, it is worth devoting time and money to getting it right. There are three main stages leading up to the interview.

- **Write a job description** for the vacant post. This may well be different from the vacated post as organizations move on and a new staff appointment is one of the most effective ways of helping the process of change. The job description, together with basic but current information about the school, will be made available to all applicants.
- **Advertise the post** in a place and at a time (not the depths of the summer vacation) that is likely to attract a wide field of suitable applicants. Occasionally it is tempting not to advertise at all when you believe you have already identified the ideal candidate and you want to save money and avoid the embarrassment of a mock interview.

However genuine the motives, this is a mistake for at least three reasons:

- It gives the impression of a conspiracy, which will do long-term damage to the morale of the staff.
- It prevents internal candidates from expressing a legitimate interest in the post, and wastes an opportunity to obtain useful clues about their future development needs.
- It seriously compromises the credibility of the candidate who is appointed without any competition.

■ **Invite a selection of applicants to interview.** You want to meet them and they will most certainly want to meet you and have an opportunity to decide if yours is the school where they want to spend the next few years or perhaps the rest of their working lives. Reducing a long list of possibles to a short list of probables (assuming you have that luxury) is not an easy task and can be done only by matching the job description against the applicants' CVs and letters of application. A telephone call (with appropriate warning) to certain candidates can also be helpful at this point, but there always remains the worrying feeling that the best candidate in the flesh, as opposed to the best candidate on paper, may not have not have been included on the short list.

The success of the interview itself depends upon three factors:

- The **candidate** must feel valued.
- The **questions** must be carefully constructed.
- The **responses** must be judiciously weighed.

The candidates

The candidates need to know enough about the organization to be able to put questions into context. The interview, then, should come as the culmination of a visit which offers a variety of opportunities to flesh out the information already received through the post or via the website. For example, the question "How would you go about improving our science examination results?" is meaningless unless the candidate has a copy of recent results, talked to some of the science teachers, seen the quality of the laboratories and so on. The candidates must be able to see the organization truly at work, warts and all.

When I was interviewed for my first headship I was immediately impressed by the calm atmosphere in the school. Not a harsh sound reached my ears; not one unruly student disturbed the tranquillity of true scholarship. Only much later did I find out that the corridors in a wide zone around the carefully chosen interview room had been put out of bounds to the students! The reality was happening somewhere else.

Overall, the candidates need to find out as much as possible about the school, and there is one simple way of knowing if their experience has been positive: those who are unsuccessful will tell you it has nonetheless been a worthwhile experience and a positive contribution to their professional development.

The questions

The interview questions require careful structuring if they are to produce useful responses and they must originate from the job description. Let us suppose, for example, that the post is concerned with building up better community relations. That will have been made clear in the advertisement and in the more detailed information sent to the applicants.

The questions will be designed to test the candidate's knowledge:

- Who do you think are the major stakeholders in the local community of this school?

as well as the candidate's key competences:

- The head of ICT is threatening to resign after her computers have apparently been damaged yet again by the evening class. How are you going to handle this?

and the candidate's experience:

- Can you describe work you have done in your current school that achieved a marked improvement in the relations with the local community?

The same core questions should be asked of every candidate, with additional questions shaped for particular individuals. Questions concerning race, religion, disability, children (as opposed to students) and age should be avoided as most of them will be illegal.

The interviewing panel will comprise those who have an immediate responsibility for the post, but I often included a more junior member of staff, for two reasons: first, because it contributes to the development of the staff member and, second, to channel feedback into a section of the staff room that sometimes feels cut off from important decision-making. Before the interview the panel will meet to agree its procedures, and after each interview it should review its performance, and one simple measure is the ratio of candidate talk to panel talk, which should be as high as possible. The panel chair will introduce each candidate to members of the panel, explain the general format of the interview so that there are no surprises, ensure that this format is followed and at the end invite the candidate's own questions. I remember putting that offer to a student applying for a place at York University. "Yes", he said, pulling out a notebook, "I had rather a long train journey so I wrote 15 questions down here so I didn't forget them." My heart sank but he got his place.

The responses
The most difficult interviewing skill is listening carefully to the candidate's answers. Often you are so busy phrasing the next question in your mind that you are not listening properly to the candidate's answer to the last question. For that reason it is worth having a panel member whose sole job is to listen and to keep notes. It is essential that someone keep notes because they could be demanded if the appointment goes wrong and is subsequently challenged in an industrial tribunal. I discouraged detailed analysis between interviews, knowing that many initial conclusions would be revised in the light of what is to follow. It can be helpful to fill in a rough score card, marking an agreed list of competences, but there is a danger of rewarding mediocrity with a safe score on each category, rather than risking a more distorted but interesting profile.

When the final interview was over I would start to seek consensus amongst the panel, asking first if some names could be dropped at once from further discussion. Could we make an immediate decision or did we need to sleep on it? At this point two dangerous temptations come into play. The first urges the appointment of the safe candidate, someone who will not rock the boat, challenge the authority of a rather weak head of department or cause embarrassment at the Parent Teachers Association cheese and wine party. The second temptation drives you to make any appointment because there is a vacancy to fill, there are students to teach and the summer vacation starts in two weeks' time. Both temptations must be resisted: no purpose is served by appointing the second best even if you suspect that the best will prove a handful to manage, and if there is doubt the appointment should not be made; the post should be readvertised and the process started again. Whatever the temporary difficulties caused by a staff vacancy, they are negligible compared with the long-term effects of making the wrong appointment.

J is for Job descriptions

Leadership is not the same as management, but the two are very closely related. If a successful leader is someone able to bring about necessary change, then a successful manager will contribute to that process by achieving defined objectives on time and on budget. Successful leaders may have a different profile of skills and experience from successful managers, but they will ensure that effective tools of management are in place, particularly basic school policies and procedures.

There is a saying "if you cannot measure it you cannot manage it". This is clearly nonsense, as much of the time it is the management of human relationships that makes a difference, and these do not fit conveniently on to a scale of 1 to 10. However, there is much to be said for "getting the measure" of something, knowing its size and bringing it under control.

The school leader is involved in a variety of rapidly changing activities during a typical day, most of them involving other people and therefore stressful, and some of them demanding immediate action. In such circumstances it can literally be a life-saver to know that important administrative procedures have already been worked on and put in place. You may not want to do it yourself but, with your encouragement, someone on your staff will enjoy the delegated task.

Job descriptions fall into this category. They do not excite me; indeed, there was a time when I would have resisted the whole notion of a detailed description of every post in the organization, but I have come to understand their importance, and I remind myself that during many difficult discussions about performance, promotion and pay I have had the reassurance of knowing exactly what the employee was expected to do, and indeed had agreed to do on signing a contract.

There are other reasons for taking job descriptions seriously.

- During moments of disagreement it is easy to confuse the job with the person who is carrying it out. An accurate job description allows us to distinguish the needs of the job from the personality of the job holder.
- At the same time it requires us to describe the qualities of the person we ideally need to perform the particular task and thus provides a vital element in staff recruitment.
- The job description is also the starting point for the process of staff appraisal and for the identification of professional development needs.
- Finally, it forms the basis of a rational system of staff remuneration based upon job classification.

Elements of a job description

Title
Make no mistake: people are often more concerned about their job's title than the job itself. Title denotes status, so be careful: director, manager, head, coordinator—each term is laden with hidden meanings that will resonate throughout the organization. You should try to be internally consistent (for example "director" should imply a different level of responsibility from "head"), but it is futile to try to tie it all in with other organizations because your head will be their principal, their coordinator will be your supervisor.

Description
This may sound obvious, but the act of writing the description of what the post is for often reveals how much has been taken for granted; the need for the post has never been properly discussed. The description should prompt the question, "Should we be doing this?" or, perhaps, "Could we be doing it in another way?" Imagine, for example, that the school has a vacancy for someone responsible for special educational needs (SEN) but that, as part of a recent policy, the school has already allocated an SEN responsibility to a teacher in each academic department. The newly vacant

role has changed; it has become one of coordination rather than direction. This must be reflected in the description.

Organizational chart

This is often called an organigram, a diagram that shows the reporting relationships between different members of staff. But many teachers in high schools wear two hats, one academic and the other pastoral, so they belong to two teams, each with a different leader. This involves the concept known as matrix management, which is a feature of many schools. It can be a recipe for tension, but tension can be a positive feature of human relationships provided the responsibilities of each team leader are made explicit and the institutional culture is one of cooperation.

> I once commissioned a parent who was a professional designer to create a three-dimensional Rubik's cube model of our matrix management. It was impressive to watch as a simple click or two transferred teachers from one team to another and back again, but I am reminded of the *New Yorker* cartoon that showed two employees studying a huge organizational chart. One is saying to the other, "I reported to the vice president of finance until someone discovered it wasn't a dotted line at all … just some spilled coffee."

Accountabilities

These are the results that are expected from the job and are what the job-holder will be held responsible for at the time of appraisal. They are best described in terms of what is done, to whom it is done and the expected outcome. The outcome should be described in terms that can be measured, not necessarily quantitatively, but in some meaningful way. Let us suppose, for example, that the job description of a history teacher requires the post-holder to teach a particular history syllabus to classes in Years 9, 10, 11 and 12. The outcomes could be described in terms of the motivation of the pupils (of which there are various measurements), their rate of choosing the subject when it becomes optional and their success in public tests and examinations as well as the vitality of the school's history club.

Knowledge, skills and experience

These should be the minimum required for the post and will not necessarily mirror those of the current post-holder. Too often, formal qualifications are overemphasized, perhaps because they are the most easily verified. Surely we should not hold people guilty of lacking this diploma, that certificate or the other degree for the rest of their professional lives. The value of qualifications declines from the very moment they are awarded, and experience (which ideally combines practice with in-service study) rapidly takes over.

> One of my few inspirational moments was to appoint a teacher who had been head of boys' physical education to become head of music. He lacked any formal musical qualification—not a single piece of paper—but he was a brilliant, instinctive musician, playing brass, string and keyboard instruments with equal skill and, more to the point, enthusing hundreds of students in the school's annual musical production. Quite quickly, with the help of the music adviser from the local education authority, he filled the gaps in his knowledge and experience and the school's music thrived under his leadership.

Behaviours

Finally, the job description will list the core behaviours that are required from the post-holder. These will usually be categorized under communication, teamwork, planning and organizing, and decision-making. These behaviours, together with the knowledge, skills and experience, will be the basis upon which decisions are made in the selection of new staff. They will also be the basis of the annual appraisal and the foundation of a rational form of remuneration that relates reward to the formal classification of the post in terms of knowledge, skills, qualifications and financial responsibility.

School leaders rarely sleep entirely soundly at night, but the knowledge that a huge administrative procedure, a description of all the different jobs in the organization, has been addressed rationally, logically and in detail can be profoundly reassuring. You have got the measure of it.

K is for Key performance indicators

Imagine you are driving along a busy road to get to an important meeting, something that even on a fine day involves a significant risk. However, you are keeping a regular watch on the car's instruments, which tell you that you are not exceeding the speed limit, that you have enough fuel for about another 200 km and that the engine is not overheating. Three important elements of risk are being regularly monitored so that you can devote your full attention to the crowded road ahead. That is the purpose of key performance indicators (KPIs): they provide a regular check on different aspects of the organization's performance so you can either relax or else take appropriate action. These are known as *diagnostic* KPIs.

Your car has another device on board, a small computer that displays the fuel consumption. This information does little to influence today's journey but it is helping you to drive the car in a more fuel-efficient way. Aware of an increasingly carbon-conscious society, you have decided to make the most effective use of the car's cruise control facility, and the fuel consumption figures are essential if you are to achieve this new goal. They provide an example of a *strategic* KPI.

There are times when the school leader feels responsible for the sins of the world and is not sure where to start to tackle them:

- disappointing examination results for the year
- defeat in the regional soccer semi-finals
- a student accused of shoplifting in the town centre
- still more delays in the renovation of the technology rooms.

It is hard to resist the temptation to blame yourself and to rush from one problem to the next either spinning plates or putting out fires. But had you known that, overall, the examination results are still far above the national average, the school has achieved the best all-round sports results for the last five years despite the soccer defeat, and the number of offending pupils reported by the police is the lowest since you started recording it, you could then focus all your energy on getting the technology rooms completed.

What you need are some facts and figures, some targets and trends, and this is where KPIs are useful. Each word is significant:

Key	they must be important
Performance	they must relate to something you can influence, where you can set targets
Indicators	they must be measurable and be truly related to the issue that concerns you.

Going back to your car journey for a moment, each variable (speed, remaining fuel and engine temperature) is evidently related to the successful completion of your journey. Each is under your control and has a set target, probably indicated by a line on a dial; each is being accurately measured. You can say with confidence 'all is as it should be'.

> When I started my first headship I compiled a list of about 15 different diagnostic KPIs. They ranged from the obvious (examination results) via the unusual (faculty short-term absence rates) to the bizarre (money spent on repairing broken windows). In each case I set targets after discussion with appropriate colleagues and I studied trends from year to year, realizing that one dipstick measurement was probably meaningless. Without argument, the most important KPI was the number of families in the town putting our school as their number one choice. If that started to slip then loud alarm bells began to ring throughout the building. I now look back at the rest of my list with a mixture of satisfaction, because this was the 1970s and I was ahead of the game, and embarrassment because I fear that some of my KPIs were meaningless.

For example, what was I trying to understand better by measuring the annual cost of window repair? Naively, I was using it as a measure of student discipline, arguing that boisterous, unsupervised behaviour inside and outside the school buildings would result in more physical damage (probably true) and that one useful measure would be broken windows (probably false). However, it did have an important indirect benefit: the caretaker was much quicker in reporting and organizing their repair. I thought I was on stronger ground using short-term absence as a measure of faculty morale. Surely the keen, motivated teacher would ignore the morning's aches and pains, get out of bed and go to school. I even set a target of 2% lost teacher-days, but I have to confess that I have since read about research that casts serious doubt on the reliability of this particular KPI.

So the choice of useful and meaningful KPIs is not easy, but there is one aspect of the above example that I did get right. I tried to reflect a wide range of the school's activities in my choice. For example, each year I measured the amount of money spent on professional development and related it to a target that was set as a percentage of the school's annual staff salary. I was therefore anticipating a much more recent concept known as the "balanced scorecard". This aims to monitor the organization from four different perspectives:

- finance
- learning and growth
- the customer
- internal processes.

The concept of "the customer" is still alien to some educators, but it is not a bad one to bear in mind when you consider the relationship between the school and the community it serves. However, customer satisfaction is difficult to measure, and I admire those schools that have found the time and the necessary expertise to send out a regular questionnaire to parents.

If you want to change the school, strategic KPIs are more important than diagnostic KPIs. As an example, let us suppose that you want to improve the uptake of modern languages in the school. Clearly, it is no use measuring examination results, as they will merely confirm what you know already—the current position is unacceptable. So what is likely to persuade more students to study more languages: better teaching, better student motivation, better resources perhaps? It still needs pinning down in more detail, to include something we can actually measure. For example, a richer programme of student exchanges with schools in other countries might be one way of improving motivation, so a strategic KPI could be "to increase the number of students taking part in exchanges by 25% each year over the next three years". This might have merit in itself, but here it is regarded as a specific means to a strategic end and is known as the "lead measure". The "lag measure" (which is the increased participation in modern languages) would be measured with different KPIs, of which examination results would, of course, be one.

Key performance indicators, then, provide a helpful management tool to measure what is happening now as well as to chart the progress you are making towards a better future. In some situations your first choices may prove to be unreliable, but in every case the discussion and debate will have been worthwhile. Moreover, KPIs will be especially helpful to busy members of the board of governors who do not have the time to dig deeply into the structure of the organization yet have an important responsibility for its overall well-being.

L is for Learning

At last we have got there! Halfway through the alphabet and we have reached the heart of the matter. Learning is what schools are for, and learning is what school leaders must lead. However far the head is from the school's day-to-day instruction, however wide the delegation of responsibility, the head is ultimately accountable for the nature and quality of the school's learning. Happily, there is no shortage of advice!

Mass school-based education is a relatively recent phenomenon, introduced over the past 150 years. It is therefore easy to follow the writings of those who have contributed to its development, and these centre around two fundamental questions:

- What is the purpose of education?
- How do young people learn most effectively?

Different leaders will be influenced by different thinkers; and they must construct a coherent educational philosophy using these thinkers' philosophies together with their own experience. Here are some of the writers who have influenced me.

A British educator

I recently bought a first edition (1861) of the essays written by the British social philosopher, Herbert Spencer, entitled *Education*. Despite the expense, I could not resist a book that opens with the key question, "What knowledge is of most worth?" Spencer complains that nobody has even bothered to ask the question, never mind propose an answer. His answer is those activities leading to:

- self-preservation
- securing the necessities of life
- the rearing of children
- the maintenance of proper social and political relations
- the gratification of tastes and feelings.

> *How to live?—that is the essential question for us. In what way to treat the body; in what way to treat the mind; in what way to manage our affairs, in what way to bring up a family; in what way to behave as a citizen; in what way to use those sources of happiness which nature supplies.*

It is stimulating, no-nonsense writing, and Spencer's development of each category reminds us how much a school curriculum reflects the thinking of its time. For Spencer, who was writing just two years after the publication of *The Origin of Species* (it was Spencer, not Darwin, who first used the phrase "the survival of the fittest"), the future lay with science.

He concludes:

> *... to the question we set out with—What knowledge is of most worth?—the uniform reply is—Science. This is the verdict on all the counts.*

And before we, with the benefit of 150 years' experience of the pluses and minuses of science, dismiss his conclusion as naive, let us take note of Spencer's warning, which strikes a special chord at the start of the 21st century:

> *But for science we should be still worshipping fetishes; or, with hecatombs of victims, propitiating diabolical deities.*

An American educator

Writing 50 years later, the philosopher and psychologist John Dewey was similarly concerned about the purpose of education.

> *What the best and wisest parent wants for his own child, that must the community want for all its children. Any other ideal for our schools is narrow and unlovely; acted upon it destroys our democracy.*

Dewey, like Spencer, was reacting to the social changes around him:

> *... the one that overshadows and even controls all others, is the industrial one—the application of science resulting in the great inventions that have utilized the forces of nature on a vast and inexpensive scale.*

If Spencer's emphasis is on the growth of the individual, Dewey's is on building the kind of society that we want those individuals to grow up in. These two concepts establish the enduring duality of education: individuality and commonality, idiosyncrasy and conformity, autonomy and solidarity.

International educators

Fast forward through most of the 20th century to some contemporary thinking that has especially impressed me: the report to the United Nations Educational, Scientific and Cultural Organization (Unesco) of the International Commission on Education for the Twenty-first Century (1996) entitled *Learning: The Treasure Within* and usually known, after its chairman, as the Delors Report. Now, the relationship between the individual and society is quoted as just one of a number of tensions to be accommodated. Since Herbert Spencer and John Dewey, the world has become a much more complex and diverse place, bringing with it the expectation of global as well as local citizenship. The Delors Report constructs global education on a foundation of four pillars:

- learning to know
- learning to do
- learning to live with others
- learning to be.

... formal education has traditionally focused mainly, if not exclusively, on learning to know and, to a lesser extent on learning to do ... The Commission believes that equal attention should be paid in all organized learning to each of these four pillars, so that education is regarded as a total experience throughout life ... focusing on both the individual and the individual's place in society.

The first fundamental question for the educational leader is, then, "For what purpose do we learn?" The second is "How do we learn most effectively?"

A Swiss educator

It is impossible to work in Geneva, as I did for nearly 15 years, without being aware of the huge influence of its most famous educator, Jean Piaget. (On reflection, he is its second most famous educator because we must not forget Jean Jacques Rousseau.) Thanks to Piaget we understand how children pass through a number of distinct cognitive development stages as their brains mature and they interact with the environment. The child assimilates experiences that are at the appropriate cognitive stage and, in gradually accommodating new experiences, is able to move to the next stage of development. Thus, the interaction of the learner with the environment creates learning that belongs to each child, rather than being "something out there".

Piaget was largely concerned with "what is", describing knowledge at different points in the child's development. Educators are more interested in "what might be"–the deliberate intervention in the learning process in order to make it more effective.

Two more American educators

No one has contributed more to our understanding of the intervention in the natural process of learning than the developmental psychologist Jerome Bruner. In his work entitled *Towards the Theory of Instruction*, Bruner describes four major features of this theory:

- It should specify the experiences that most encourage the child to learn (the relationship with the teacher, for example).
- It should specify the best way of structuring knowledge to make it accessible to the learner (for example, the periodic table does more than just list the elements; it does so in a way that enables the learner to generate new knowledge).

- It should specify the most effective way of sequencing knowledge (for example, does one present a general theory and deduce its consequences or lead up to the theory from particular examples?).
- It should specify the nature and pacing of rewards and punishments (gradually moving away from extrinsic to intrinsic rewards).

Bruner presents the teacher with an uncompromising challenge when he suggests that:

We begin with the hypothesis that any subject can be taught effectively in some intellectually honest form to any child at any stage of development.

Just as the "why" of education will change to respond to the social and economic conditions of the times, so the "how" of education will be influenced by our developing knowledge of the brain and its interaction with the environment. The work of Harvard professor Howard Gardner on multiple intelligences is important in this context, and his proposal for an education based upon five minds for the globalized future, the disciplined, synthesizing, creating, respectful and ethical minds, sets up an important signpost into the 21st century.

A Chinese educator
One cannot help going back 3,000 years to link Gardner's ethical and respectful minds to the writings of Confucius:

Those in official positions should be loyal to the king, respect his lord, show concern for the people and solicitation for children and elderly.

One of Confucius's students reported:

The master instructed us in four aspects: culture, moral conduct, wholehearted sincerity and truthfulness.

and we are reminded that in different parts of the world different systems have placed different emphases on the purpose of education but none has ever neglected the moral development of the future citizen. The education of "the good person" has consistently taken precedence over "the productive person", "the authoritative person" and the "creative person".

This is a very brief glimpse at the writings of a few of those who have influenced my own thinking. Our study of learning continues, particularly as our understanding of neuroscience becomes more refined and begins to influence mainstream learning as well as offer more effective education for those with brain disorders. A school exists for the single purpose of learning, and the leader who is unable to maintain an on-going debate about its "why" and its "how" is ill prepared for the challenge of educational leadership.

M is for Making things happen

Every year during my time in Geneva my performance was analysed in a 360-degree appraisal. Those who knew my work were asked to respond, using an "always to never" scale, to about 60 statements describing various aspects of my leadership. For me (and, I suspect, for them too) one item stood out above all the others in its importance. It was Item 3 and it went as follows:

- converts vision into action: makes things happen.

This is the item that distinguishes leadership from management: leaders innovate rather than improve, they create rather than mend: they make things happen. So what practical, realistic options are available to help? What are the leadership equivalents of those huge levers that the signalmen pushed and pulled to send the next train safely down another track, in a new direction, towards a different destination? I suggest these are:

- people with the skills to work with new ideas
- money to afford them
- detailed plans to implement them

- and, where appropriate, outside advice to support and critique the new ideas.

People

I have emphasized elsewhere (pages 40 and 43) the crucial importance of making the highest quality appointments of new staff. Every vacant post presents an opportunity to do something different, to move the situation away from the status quo. However, vacancies rarely arise where and when you want them, so the capacity for making things happen lies overwhelmingly with your existing staff. They are your most precious resource and their INSET (in-service training) or CPD (continuing professional development), or whatever new acronym describes their professional development, is one of the leader's most important responsibilities.

Alas, the leader rarely sets a good example in this respect, using a variety of dubious excuses (too busy to leave school, no suitable courses available, much too expensive, other colleagues with more pressing needs and so on) to avoid a course, a conference or a seminar.

> I must confess to being a conference phobic, and I have rarely sat through a conventional conference lasting more than a day. I am sure that the fault is mine, but how rarely have I returned encouraged and inspired from these occasions. They are so undemanding of the participants, who sit there being talked at, in marked contrast to a weekend's seminar I once attended, where a group of school leaders, under the mentorship of a distinguished journalist, actually wrote the first draft of a book between Friday evening and Sunday lunchtime.
>
> I believe I have acquired more useful ideas and greater intellectual stimulus from sources outside education. In the UK I learned a huge amount through my industrial contacts with ICI, Rank-Xerox and BP. The same was true in Geneva, where I shamelessly exploited the contacts offered by different members of school's governing body, who worked for the United Nations, the World Health Organization, Dupont and CERN. Educational leadership is too important to leave entirely in the hands of educators.

Money

Change costs money, at least in the initial stages, but eventually it may bring important savings. Given the substantial fixed costs of delivering "business as usual" (in most schools the staffing alone accounts for around 75% of expenditure) every opportunity should be taken to find ways of improving cost-effectiveness.

This may involve:

- the use of new technologies, especially in reducing costs of communication
- retraining staff in order to maintain their most effective contribution
- outsourcing some of the school's services to organizations that can deliver similar quality more cheaply
- seeking economies of scale—for example, avoiding unnecessary choice in the curriculum, which produces small uneconomic teaching groups.

As well as making the best use of existing income, most schools are searching for new sources of funding. These may come from governments seeking to promote a new initiative or else from the school's own fundraising efforts. Whatever their origin they should be treated with caution because they can stimulate expectations that cannot be funded in the long term. Most capital expenditure—on buildings and equipment, for example—needs to be sustained from operating expenditure and items proudly donated by the PTA can quickly become a drain on basic funding streams.

The International Baccalaureate was given a substantial donation from the Goldman Sachs Foundation to assist the development of its ground-breaking online curriculum centre. The development needed people, experts in distance learning, and they were duly appointed, necessarily on short-term contracts. Three years later, as the grant came to an end, the experts had become an integral part of the enlarged and improved system. Fortunately, the rapid expansion of the organization enabled us to maintain their appointments from an increased operating budget. Otherwise, the entire project might easily have unwound.

Detailed planning

New initiatives need working on, shaping and refining before they can be made to happen. A huge amount of work separates a proposal from its eventual implementation, and much of that work must be done in committees and working groups. I cannot imagine a school that does not have several such groups in operation, some of them permanent standing committees. The composition of a working group will often determine its success. Never ask for volunteers because you will simply recruit all those in favour of the change; none of the counter-arguments will be explored and the recommendations will not survive the scrutiny of the first staff meeting. Make clear (indeed, publish) the remit of the working group, the timescale of its work and its relationship to the final decision. Are you asking the group to clarify, to advise or to decide?

Much unhappiness can be traced to misunderstandings about what a group has been charged to do. I can remember a school social committee that was chaired by a formidable, experienced and much-loved teacher approaching her retirement. She saw the committee as the means to make her mark, and under her forceful leadership, the social committee, whose real task it was to plan the Christmas dinner and send flowers and get-well cards to sick colleagues, somehow found itself in the front line of the school's decision-making. Its inappropriate ambitions to change the school curriculum were eventually thwarted, but not without some unnecessary frustration.

Outside advice

Sometimes a school will lack the necessary expertise within its own community and will seek to employ a consultant. Consultants should be selected and appointed with great care because they come very easily and depart rather reluctantly. In between they charge very high fees and often earn them by recycling your own ideas.

The International Baccalaureate's strategic planning exercise with the management consultants McKinsey and Co. was an outstanding exception to this rule. The secret of its success was that it satisfied six basic rules of consultancy:

1   We were clear what we needed.
2   They were prepared to listen and learn.
3   The board of governors was committed to its involvement.
4   We worked closely together throughout the two-year period of the project.
5   Both sides were prepared to be flexible and adapt to new ideas.
6   It provided exceptional intellectual stimulus to both partners.

But the most important, the most elusive, ingredient is missing: the capacity to convince, to persuade, to win over the sceptics and the doubters. This is a combination of two critical leadership qualities, credibility and communication: the leader must be able to explain the proposed change in ways that will persuade colleagues to buy into it. The tipping point will be reached when the initiative is shared and others start thinking about it, arguing about it and gradually assuming ownership for its implementation.

Unfortunately, there is another kind of tipping point, and nothing is more depressing than to see a hard-won initiative begin to falter. The school leader's task can sometimes seem like that of Sisyphus, King of Corinth, who was condemned to roll a heavy boulder to the summit of the mountain only to see it slip back again. Implementing change requires constant vigilance, and I made a discipline of revisiting my annual objectives on the same day of every month and writing to myself, and to the chair of governors, a memo about their progress, or lack of it. In this way I was forced to confront the biggest leadership challenge of all: making things happen.

N is for Nimbleness

I spent 15 very happy years working in Switzerland, arguably one of the most efficient nations in the world. In Switzerland things work as they are designed to work and they very rarely go wrong. But when they do go wrong the result can be chaotic.

One day I arrived in a hurry at Geneva airport's long-stay car park to find it full. As I arrived a car drove out and the barrier on my side lifted unexpectedly, allowing me to drive in. I parked, realized I had no ticket but, never mind, I could explain at the airport office. Alas, I was unable to explain anything because there was total denial that the system had broken down. My car simply could not be parked in a car park that had been reported full all morning. Defending the system was more important than accepting, exceptionally, that the system had gone wrong, even when it meant an angry queue of delayed travellers building up behind me. Switzerland is efficient but it is not nimble.

All organizations make mistakes. The nimble organization quickly realizes that something has gone wrong and takes appropriate remedial action while there is still time.

In the aftermath of the devastating tsunami in December 2004, the International Baccalaureate was swift to react, and within a day or two an appeal for funds was launched. Within the next day or two we realized that the wrong appeal had been launched: none of the International Baccalaureate World Schools had been directly involved and the major charities were already active and better equipped to collect funds. Instead, a revised and much more effective proposal was floated, creating supportive partnerships between affected schools and International Baccalaureate World Schools. Thus was born the School-to-School partnership project, which today includes several hundred schools and is being expanded to countries that were not affected by the tsunami.

The International Baccalaureate initiative displays several of the characteristics of nimbleness. We were quick to admit our initial mistake; we were quick to recognize the merits of an alternative scheme; we were quick to second a colleague from our Singapore office who had all the necessary qualities and experience; we were quick to set up a small but effective coordination team led by a director, who was quick to accept a responsibility that was not part of his job description.

Quickness of response is important, but a nimble organization needs more qualities than speed. Perhaps the most important are the capacity to recognize an opportunity and the desire to seize it. This will often involve an element of risk, and I realized at the time that our tsunami response was a risky business. Our Singapore colleague was frequently in the front line of some potentially dangerous situations, particularly in Aceh, and his financial negotiations with governments and other non-government organizations in the field could not conform to our customary procedures. However, we assessed the risk, found it acceptable, and gradually built in procedures to reduce it.

Clarity is another essential ingredient of nimbleness, and this is particularly true of communication. The early days of the School-to-School project depended crucially on weekly telephone conferences that brought together a dozen or so people in America, Europe and Asia. Depending on the local time of day, some would be in their offices, some at home near bedtime, while others would be on mobile phones in airports or in the field. Modern techniques of communication have transformed an organization's response time, particularly the handheld wireless devices that allow worldwide email access to mobile workers.

Clarity of another kind is important. I have mentioned elsewhere the young teacher who represented the school at an important social services case conference (see page 24). This was a nimble response because she knew the student in question far better than I did, but it was feasible only because she did not need extensive briefing on what to do, what to say and how to say it. I could trust her to negotiate the best outcome for the student because, in the end, there was a shared clarity of mission. I knew the teacher would never step outside the boundary of the school's values.

A good example of a clumsy organization occurred when a request was made to the International Baccalaureate's finance committee for an additional warehouse for storing examination scripts. The project had been carefully researched and costed but, fatally, I began to have doubts during the actual presentation. Surely, as more examination marking was done electronically our need for storage space would decline; we were trying to save pounds and spend dollars so why was the warehouse located in Cardiff rather than the United States; could we not negotiate a shorter lease with a better opt-out clause? My doubts (all of which had been anticipated in the study phase and could have been answered by the project team had I bothered to ask them) spread around the table. It was the beginning of a long period of ill-tempered exchanges, half-formed new proposals and general drift, thanks to the seeds of doubt that I had so foolishly sown. The fault was entirely mine.

In summary, a nimble organization is not one that acts on a whim or the spur of the moment. Nimbleness is the capacity to respond appropriately to the changing environment. In the case of the educational environment the appropriate response will sometimes be to wait, or do nothing, as most educational stakeholders value stability rather than revolution. A nimble organization does not abandon its strategic plan "to pursue every hare that crosses its path". Rather it measures the value of new initiatives in terms of the likely achievement of its mission and its long-term goals. Nimbleness requires, on the one hand, highly competent professional staff who are empowered to take quick and effective decisions. But on the other hand, these staff must be part of a corporate team that shares the mission and the values of the organization. Without these two basic ingredients, nimbleness quickly becomes confusion.

There are occasions when individuals have to be nimble, too. I had been invited to a school in Charlotte, North Carolina, and during the day the invitation was extended to include a reception that evening to mark the achievements of outstanding students in the district's senior high schools. As I relaxed in the front row, local dignitaries sitting next to me got up to introduce the city, the district, the schools, the teachers and the students.

Each was commendably (and unusually) brief, explaining how important it was to leave plenty of time for the distinguished guest speaker. As the final speaker rose, the awful truth began to dawn: I was the only one left in the row, which meant I must be the distinguished guest speaker and I had three minutes without paper and pencil to put together a coherent address for the next half-hour.

O is for Optimism

It takes great courage to see the world in all its tainted glory and still to love it.

So wrote Oscar Wilde in 1895, and the demands on that courage have further increased during the intervening century. I believe this poses a particular challenge for teachers, who need to embrace an act of faith that insists that the future will be better than the present and very much better than the past. It is no coincidence that during the twentieth century educational reform in the UK was associated with the tail end of war. In 1902 (the Boer war), in 1918 (the first world war) and again in 1944 (the second world war) the major building blocks of state secondary education were put into place, each new piece of legislation reflecting a country still at war but looking forward to a better future that would be the only justification for the appalling human sacrifice.

My debt to my friend and past headmaster, Harry Rée, has been evident elsewhere in this volume (see page 35), but nowhere do I feel his influence more strongly than here, within the theme of optimism. Harry had a powerful faith in humankind in general, and in young people in particular, and I shall never forget his advice to me as a young teacher: "when you meet a new class for the first time, assume that they are better than you are and will achieve more and go further than you have ever dreamt of; only then will you create the right relationship." Alas, too much of the daily exchange in schools today, mirroring the example of much of the media, is an underestimate of future potential and a demeaning of young talent: an all-round "dumbing down".

We must maintain our faith in the infinite possibilities of the next generation while recognizing that the future they face will be increasingly complex and challenging, and only by encouraging young people to deploy their talents to the full will those challenges be met. History tells us that every generation perceives unparalleled difficulties ahead, so let us be cautious about presenting the 21st century as the make-or-break century for humankind. Yet one wonders whether the customary process of extrapolating from present experiences to future expectations has ever been more unreliable because of the gathering pace of globalization.

In order to remain optimistic about the capacities of young people we must also remain optimistic about the significance of their education. In *The Great Learning*, written 2,500 years ago, Confucius had no doubts:

The ancients who wished to illustrate virtues throughout the kingdom first regulated well their own states. Wishing to order well their states, they first regulated their families. Wishing to regulate their families, they first cultivated their persons. Wishing to cultivate their persons, they first rectified their hearts. Wishing to rectify their hearts, they first sought to be sincere in their thoughts. Wishing to be sincere in their thoughts they first extended to the utmost their knowledge. Such extension of knowledge lay in the investigation of things.

Aristotle, living in a very different society but at roughly the same time, was asked how much educated men were superior to uneducated men and replied, "As much as the living are to the dead." Nearer to our times, the English Victorian poet and literary critic Matthew Arnold insisted that education for the new middle classes would mean "provincialism dissipated, its intolerance cured, its pettinesses purged away". Arnold was urging administrators to think beyond their own back yard (he was much influenced by his visit in 1859 to schools in France), thereby laying the foundation of today's concept of a global citizen.

Seeing people thinking beyond their own back yard is one of the most exciting features of international education.

I remember visiting Jim Hill High School in Jackson, Mississippi. A more socially deprived school would be difficult to imagine, and it seemed entirely appropriate that to reach it you were forced to drive through the local cemetery. But, once inside, you met two remarkable African American ladies, the principal and district superintendent, who were using the International Baccalaureate Diploma Programme to transform the school's learning, its ambitions and its reputation. Already the campus was dotted with mushrooming classrooms built to house the rapidly growing number of students.

I met this remarkable couple on several future occasions at conferences and workshops and I saw their mutually reinforcing optimism spreading contagiously to those around them. Yes, eventually they might admit they did lack this or that, there had been some disappointments, one or two things had not quite worked out as they had hoped. But this was against a background of shared optimism; not a thin veneer of goodwill and vain hope but a deep-seated conviction that their school was starting to belong to the world. And indeed it was, and Jim Hill's wonderful choir was invited to Washington to sing at the memorial service following 9/11.

The link between education and conflict prevention is a recent one. The prologue to the 1945 Charter of Unesco makes the connection clear with the famous words attributed to the American poet Archibald MacLeish:

Since wars begin in the minds of men, it is in the minds of men that the defences of peace must be constructed.

Kofi Annan, former Secretary General of the United Nations, described education as "peace keeping by another name", but can we be confident that we are promoting a style of education that is likely to achieve this aim? The mission statement of the International Baccalaureate commits to developing "... caring young people who help to create a better and more peaceful world ...", and the organization has devoted much time and thought to the content and the process of an appropriate education, but even this, in the end, contains a large measure of optimistic faith.

To be of any practical value, optimism must be backed up by action or it will be rendered platitudinous.

When I was seconded to ICI its chairman was the charismatic John Harvey-Jones. Interviewed on the radio, he was asked rather aggressively what he proposed to do when his company had used up the world's entire supply of a particular rare metal—I forget which. "Oh," he replied, without a moment's hesitation, "we'll change our manufacturing processes so we can use something else." His response scored zero for political correctness, but it illustrates perfectly my point that optimism must be linked to appropriate action.

Globalization is radically changing the environment in which schools are operating. Yet there is little indication that anyone has noticed, and education remains one of the least studied dimensions of globalization. I would feel more optimistic about the future if young people were being educated to face the challenges of this century rather than those of the last. Globalization brings benefits and threats. Its potential for good and for evil needs to be understood by young people, who (unlike my generation) will always live in a globalized world. But understanding is not enough: action must follow, and this will demand unusual combinations of competences: entrepreneurialism and community service; local and global participation; understanding one's own culture as a bridge to respecting the cultures of others; critical thinking skills linked to compassion. To borrow the phrase of the eminent American writer Thomas Friedman, we shall need young people who can combine "business school heads with social worker hearts".

It is essential that optimism for the future be kept alive in schools because if not there then where else? But its focus will have to change because we can no longer promise material improvement, at least in the developed world. Instead, our optimism is built upon the conviction that the next generation will be able to respond positively to the enormous challenges of global conflict, disease and climate change that will confront it as, in every sense, the planet shrinks. The educational leader must be optimistic and accept a clear responsibility to provide a style of education that justifies that optimism.

P is for Playing by the rules

Research suggests that the leader's most respected quality is credibility. Leaders are judged by their words, but, more importantly, by their deeds—can the leader be believed and trusted? An essential component of credibility is consistency, and in an organization like a school that comes from playing by the rules.

> I remember an experienced teacher at the International School of Geneva, for whom I had enormous respect, saying to me after a particularly controversial decision: "I never expected you to behave like that." I will come to the reason for his comment in a moment, but it remains fresh in my mind because it hurt at the time and it still hurts today. It called into question my consistency and my credibility; how would I behave the next time?

Three sets of rules guide a school and a wise school leader will be alert to all of them:

- laws of the country in which the school is located
- relationships between employer and employee
- traditions and conventions peculiar to the institution.

Laws of the country

These laws will set the framework for acceptable child–adult relationships, for *in loco parentis* responsibilities, financial procedures, health and safety regulations, the prevention of discrimination by age, gender and race and so on. They will often be complex in interpretation, and every school should have ready access to expert legal advice. However, prevention is better than cure and, in increasingly litigious societies, the judicious school leader will think each major decision through to its worst-scenario legal conclusions, remembering that, in the end, justice may be done but at a very considerable cost to the school. Whenever I spoke to a lawyer I reminded myself of the very expensive clock ticking in the background and I forbade any member of staff to seek legal advice on the school's behalf without my prior approval. This was a responsibility that I rarely delegated.

Professional relationships

In many countries these will be determined nationally, but in most situations there will still be flexibility for some local interpretation. How many working days? How many staff meetings? What about home leave in an international school? What contractual safeguards does the teacher have? What are the obligations for meeting parents? I have explained elsewhere (page 40) how I came to favour a set of rules that left as little as possible to individual interpretation, as little as possible to voluntary goodwill. In Geneva, for example, the rules were contained in the *Convention Collective*, which in turn was based upon Swiss Federal law contained in the so-called *Code des Obligations*. The former was regularly renegotiated, along with salaries, and the latter was never far from my desk.

The three schools of which I was head could be described as "heavily unionized". The phrase has sinister overtones, but it simply means that the staff–teachers and non-teaching–were mostly members of professional associations whose elected representatives looked after their interests as employees of the school. I found this unthreatening, and I usually enjoyed working with the union representatives, who were not only honest and straightforward in their dealings with me but were also unusually conscientious and talented teachers. I doubt that this was coincidental: teachers want their views to be understood and defended by colleagues who not only are competent negotiators, but are professionally respected as teachers. I kept the "union reps" fully informed about issues that were likely to affect them, holding a regular weekly meeting rather than waiting for a crisis to arise. Occasionally I would talk to them off the record about a particularly sensitive issue, and this confidentiality was never abused.

In the mid-1980s, in what was one of the most challenging periods of my school leadership, some of the conventional rules were deliberately suspended by the national teachers' unions in an attempt to force the UK government of the day to improve salaries and conditions of service. Interestingly, it was called a "work to rule", and it meant that participation in all voluntary activities (which was interpreted to include after-school meetings with parents) was withdrawn. The situation lasted several months and meant that we had to adjust to a new set of rules. However, because relationships with the union reps in the school were so positive, we were able to minimize the damage to the school, and in some respects we emerged from the experience strengthened, particularly in terms of our communication with parents.

Traditions and conventions

Casting these aside is a high-risk strategy for any leader, and sensitivity towards these usually unwritten laws is often one of the severest tests of a new school head. Everyone watches a new leader.

> As part of the 70th birthday celebrations at the International School of Geneva, I decided that students from both campuses should graduate together in the United Nations building in Geneva, the famous Palais des Nations, and I arranged for a distinguished United Nations official to address the ceremony. One campus was not at all pleased: its students wished to graduate from its famous Greek Theatre, from which their brothers, sisters, cousins, parents, uncles and aunts had graduated over the years. By sheer luck the resulting impasse was resolved when the distinguished United Nations official was suddenly summoned to Rwanda and I was able to back down, not losing too much face and gaining some important experience about the strength of local traditions.

So what had provoked that colleague to accuse me of untypical behaviour? I had decided to bend the rules in order to terminate the contract of a mathematics teacher who was generally deemed to be hopeless. Everyone in the school's community knew that he was hopeless but, predictably, there was not a scrap of evidence to support this view in his file. Fearing the continuation of widespread damage to his students' learning, I decided to act and to act rather quickly, not actually breaking any rules but certainly compressing the timescale within which they were designed to operate. At the time, I strongly believed that my action, taken in the best interests of the students, was justified. In retrospect, I think that any short-term gain was probably outweighed by the damage done to more important long-term relationships within the school. I have no doubt, too, that my decision was influenced by increasing external pressure from parents, board members and the students themselves and appearing to give in to them established an unhelpful precedent for the future.

Playing strictly by the rules can be a frustrating and a time-consuming business. It is therefore tempting to break them, if only to remind those around you of your authority but, as Bertrand Russell tells us in his "A Liberal Decalogue", a victory dependent upon authority is likely to be unreal and illusory. Bending the rules, as I have illustrated, can be equally damaging to your reputation amongst those whose opinion you particularly value. Side-stepping the rules rarely works either. For example, in many bureaucratic societies it is often a relatively junior staff member who frustrates your best-laid plans, often for no other reason than to exert petty authority. Why not avoid the problem by negotiating directly with that person's superior (whom you perhaps happen to know socially)? This is invariably a mistake. The superior will, of course, agree and then ask the intermediary to carry out the necessary action. So do not be surprised when nothing happens, and next time play by the rules!

Q is for Questioning beliefs

The head of a school has considerable power and influence, though perhaps not as much as Winston Churchill envied when he remarked: "headmasters have powers at their disposal with which Prime Ministers have never been invested." Other people listen seriously to school leaders, and opinion polls continue to confirm that they are widely regarded as reliable and uncorrupted. This makes it even more important that the leaders are prepared to admit that they sometimes get it wrong, and I once suggested to an audience of heads that they should have prominently displayed on their desks the famous admonition of Oliver Cromwell: "I beseech you in the bowels of Christ think it possible you may be mistaken."

I am not thinking of the inevitable misjudgments, mistakes and misunderstandings that are a feature of any seriously demanding job, but rather of the doubts and shifts of mind on more fundamental issues that have hitherto underpinned one's professional values. It is not easy to change your mind, to admit you have been wrong and in an activity like education, where passions run high and most people have an opinion, questioning fundamental beliefs can be portrayed as the prelude to changing sides, an early symptom of betrayal.

I am going to describe three examples where, during a career of some 40 years, I changed my mind not because I had been wrong, but because I believed I was no longer right. Each case prompts the question "Why?"

Was it some Damascene conversion? Did someone persuade me? Was it short-term expediency? Was I blown by the wind of public opinion? Why did I do it?

Access to opportunity

I started teaching in a very academic boys' grammar school, and I am glad I did because, despite the school's rather laid-back attitude to its staff, the experience set me lifelong benchmarks for measuring what motivated students can achieve when teachers set them challenging targets. I doubt that I shall ever teach such a rewarding class as my first tutor group—I can still remember all their names. If that were not enough, I had an outstanding role model in my first head of department. But, by the time I left, doubts had set in about the way these boys had been chosen, and my next appointment, as a university lecturer in education, helped to confirm my change of mind about grammar school selection and reinforce my belief in the rapidly developing comprehensive school system. Five years later, to the general astonishment of my colleagues, I gave up my tenured university post in favour of the deputy headship at Carisbrooke High School, a huge, challenging comprehensive school. It was one of the best decisions I ever made.

Access to learning

The question of access—which students should have the right to which kind of education—has dominated my career. Selection, equal opportunities, academic versus vocational courses, special educational needs—these are all fundamental issues which determine the life chances of young people. At this time—I am talking about the mid-1970s in the UK—comprehensive schools were large, almost by definition, so as to generate the economies of scale that would sustain the variety of curriculum choice that satisfied the new variety of student. Choice was the motto of comprehensive education: each to his or her own chosen subject so that opportunities were maximized. So it was with eager anticipation that I went to Carisbrooke, which had more than 400 students in each year group, and it was with some astonishment that I found that there was virtually no choice at all. My second conversion was about to take place, to the concept of a "common curriculum": all students were required to study the same basic academic subjects (though not at the same level) and choice was deliberately limited before the Years 11 and 12. Carisbrooke was leading a growing movement that would culminate a decade later in the UK National Curriculum, but at the time it was a controversial policy that needed firm leadership from the head to sustain and develop it.

Access to international education

In 1990 I went back to South Africa, where I had been a graduate student at the University of Cape Town exactly 25 years earlier. It was a period of dramatic change between the release from prison of Nelson Mandela and the formation of a democratically elected government. I had been commissioned to write a number of articles for the *Times Educational Supplement*, and this, together with my personal contacts, gave me the reason and the opportunity to visit a number of black and white schools. Amidst all the uncertainty, two things were clear: the black education system was in terminal decline, deliberately undermined as a symbol of apartheid by the African National Congress. At the same time the white state schools were trying to come to terms with a future that would be very different and very difficult.

Unexpectedly, it was a third group of schools that I found the most interesting, the independent schools. Many of them had an international mix of students, and in defiance of the laws of apartheid they had kept a window open on the rest of the world at a time when South Africa had been virtually isolated by economic and political sanctions. For the first time I understood that in some situations independent education can be very important indeed. I also began to understand the limitations of a national education. On arrival back home I applied for the post in Geneva, and so started my involvement in international education and my commitment to the education of global, as well as national, citizens.

What makes people change their minds? The Harvard psychologist Howard Gardner has identified seven R factors:

- reason
- research
- resonance (a gut feeling)
- redescription (being able to describe the change in several different forms)
- resources and rewards
- real world events
- resistances.

So, for example, the factors behind my increasing unease about grammar schools certainly included research proving the unreliability of selection tests as well as the likelihood of better rewards and more resources in a rapidly expanding comprehensive system. My commitment to international education can be linked to a knowledge of real world events and reasoning about the consequences of globalization.

It is interesting to link Gardner's seven factors to Gleicher's formula (see page 22). Gardner is concerned with reasons for change, Gleicher with the process of change, but there is an overlap, and the most effective leaders will think synchronously about the "why" and the "how" of the change.

Good leaders will quickly develop a strong resonance, a network of belief that is shaped by an all-round awareness of the way the world is going. Whether this resonance persuades them to go along with the rest of the world or to take a stand against it is perhaps the toughest aspect of leadership. At what point does personal conviction collide with corporate policy? Do school leaders have the right to use the status of their position and the authority of their school to support a particular cause? Are school leaders really the drivers or merely the ticket collectors? These are all issues of which resignations are made.

R is for Risk management

Nothing ventured, nothing gained. Look before you leap. A bird in the hand is worth two in the bush. Better safe than sorry. Better the devil you know. Out of the frying pan into the fire ...

The huge number of proverbs that describe the dangers of risk reminds us how large it has always loomed in our lives. Risk concerns those elements of our lives that are not entirely predictable either because they are not fully understood or because they are not fully under our control. Every day we venture into an unknown where aircraft still crash, people die of AIDS-related diseases and businesses go bankrupt. But we live in a society that is becoming more risk averse, believing it to be a malevolent feature of an uncivilized age, so there is a strong temptation to leave unexplored those areas of our lives that are not fully understood or fully under control. If we get too close they might bite us.

Unfortunately, taking risks is an inescapable prelude to learning, and you are never too young to take one. The International Baccalaureate's Primary Years Programme, for example, specifically encourages risk-takers who:

... approach unfamiliar situations and uncertainty with courage and

forethought and have the independence of spirit to explore new roles,
ideas and strategies.

It's hard to disagree with that, and I remember asking a young girl in an
elementary school in America what this meant for her. Well, she replied,
I reckon every time I put up my hand to answer a question in my French
class I take a risk! Risk-taking is part of the process of growing up, as
parents come to understand all too well when they hand over the car keys
just hours after their son or daughter has passed his or her driving test.

So we have a conundrum to resolve because, on the one hand, taking
risks can hurt, can indeed be fatal; but, on the other hand, if we don't
take them we don't learn and we don't grow up. The answer lies in
understanding the risk, measuring it and trying to manage it. We need to
start with an acceptable definition of risk, but first we should remember
that research shows how the willingness to take risks is one of those social
characteristics that distinguish one culture from another. Thus, the French
are much more likely to try to avoid uncertainty in their lives than the
British; the Japanese more than the Americans.

> In Geneva my Francophone colleagues, and especially board members,
> were often deeply suspicious of my occasional, and typically British, "well
> let's give it a go" approach when they would feel comfortable only with a
> carefully argued, detailed proposal supported by copious evidence, before
> setting off into the unknown. On reflection this may go some way towards
> explaining my perception of a dysfunctional board.

A widely used definition of an unacceptable risk is one that in the
worst case will adversely affect the organization's strategic plan or
damage the organization's reputation. A widely used measurement of risk
divides it into two components, its likely impact and its likely occurrence
(note the "likely"–there is a strongly subjective element here) and awards
each component a score out of five. Thus, the resignation of your loyal
deputy head may score 5 for impact but only 1 for likelihood, whereas
bad behaviour on the buses might score 2 for impact but 5 for likelihood.
Multiplying the two gives an overall risk factor and a decision can then
be taken to manage every risk with a factor greater than a chosen figure,
say 20.

What do we mean by "managing risk"? First we need to write it down,
with its risk factor, in a risk register. Then different people who have
an appropriate responsibility must be assigned to look after each of the
selected risks and to propose ways in which they can be minimized.

Finally, each risk in the register should be reported on regularly to the school's senior management team and, in the most serious cases, to the board of governors. All this may sound rather heavy-handed, but one of the biggest leadership worries is dealing with the unknown, and the adage "what cannot be measured cannot be managed" can sometimes be a helpful warning. Some problems—substance abuse is one of them—will never be solved, never put to bed, never be taken off the agenda. So I found great reassurance when dealing with uncertainty in getting a feel of the size of the problem, even if there was no immediate remedy for it. Do we have two serious risks, 20 or 200? We need to know, and we need to feel confident that planned action is being taken.

On the whole, schools are not places of high drama, but once in a while a more risky situation occurs.

An oil engineer returned from Africa with his Nigerian wife and, so they said, her 16 year-old nephew. The boy was duly enrolled and he quickly became fully involved in the life of the school, particularly its sport and music. He was an excellent student and a fine role model in a school that had relatively few non-white faces. Over the months it became clear to us that the story of his origins was false and he was in fact an illegal immigrant. Should we play by the rules and blow the whistle? I'm afraid we did everything possible to thwart the course of justice until he had successfully taken his GCSE examinations and when the police car eventually arrived I was not sure if it was for him or for me.

In Geneva there were risks of another kind, and no sooner had I arrived than I was attending the funeral of a member of staff who had been killed in a climbing accident. Every weekend we had school minibuses transporting students here, there and everywhere, often into potentially dangerous environments. While we took every possible precaution to minimize the risks we knew that, statistically, one day disaster would strike, so we also asked ourselves the very practical question "What if?" and designed a simulation of a fatal minibus accident. We produced a disaster contingency plan—how would we ensure that information was accurate, inform parents, deal with the press—which, happily, we never had to put into operation during my time at the school. In a different way we were trying to measure and respond to the unknown or, in this case, to the unthinkable.

But it is the small, everyday risks that are the real challenge to a school. Helping students to risk embarrassment in a public presentation, helping them to risk injury in a physical sport, to risk failure in an ambitious university application or to risk misunderstanding in an conversation in a foreign language—these are some of the everyday challenges for teachers, yet our increasingly litigious society requires us to focus all our energy on their elimination. In my experience, people can be divided into two broad groups: those who say "yes" to a challenge and then face up to the sometimes risky consequences and those who say "no" and never learn what the exciting consequences might have been.

S is for Strategic planning

Nothing is more important for the future health of an organization than its strategic plan, except perhaps the process that produced the plan. A strategic plan is a road map that will last for several years—probably more than five but less than ten—to help you get from where you are now to where you want to be. Without it:

- You will squander time and resources going down minor roads.
- You will fail to notice that a whole section of your preferred route has been shut off for repairs.
- You may even perish when your vehicle drives over a cliff.

The success of strategic planning depends upon how well you understand your present position, how clearly you can visualize your future position and how accurately you can predict what will lie in between.

There is no single, preferred method of preparing a strategic plan. I have been closely involved in three—one at the International School of Geneva and two at the International Baccalaureate—and each was done differently.

- The first was a powerful bottom-up exercise with very extensive (arguably excessive) community initiative and involvement.

- The second had a much lighter touch, was largely constructed by me in its first draft and then put out for consultation.
- The third involved 18 months' intensive work carried out for free by international management consultants McKinsey and Co.

In retrospect I would rate them, respectively, as too heavy, too light and about right.

The process of strategic planning can be divided into several steps: prepare the mission statement, assess the current position, undertake an environmental scan, ask where you want to be, focus on a limited number of strategic goals, break each goal into objectives and then put it all into practice.

Mission statement

What does the school stand for? What is it trying to achieve? What is its mission? This, if you like, defines the purpose of the journey: never mind the route, what is the point in going there? It needs to be brief, to be inspiring and to provide guidance when choices arise. The mission statement of the International Baccalaureate, which we struggled to get right for over a year, is all three and, as a bonus, it has been controversial and provocative. By contrast, the mission statement of the International School of Geneva was too vague:

> *We aim to provide an education which anticipates the future needs of our students, helping them to acquire the necessary skills and motivation to continue learning and lead a fulfilled life.*

Well, yes, but what skills, what kind of education and what kind of future? Invest time in getting the mission statement right because you will come back to it again and again; it is at the core of the process.

Assess where the school is now

I find a **SWOT** analysis, carried out by the different stakeholders, the most practical way of approaching this. What are the current **Strengths** and **Weaknesses** and, in the context of the local and national scene, what are its biggest **Opportunities** and most serious **Threats?** How can you build upon your opportunities and minimize the threats? What is likely to happen in five years' time (this is a tough question to answer) if you carry on just as you are now?

Environmental scan

This is probably best done by someone outside the school. What is the world going to look like over the next five to ten years? What are likely to be the major changes that will impact upon the life of your school? No one knows precisely, but then strategic planning does not pretend to be an exact science. The consultant commissioned to do the scan in Geneva identified four major messages about the future, one of which (not as obvious at the time as it is now) was the increasing relevance of international education for the school's local Swiss and French community. McKinsey went about its International Baccalaureate scan with a characteristic combination of panache and precision. How many students worldwide would be able to study an International Baccalaureate programme (answer: about 90 million); what advantages would the International Baccalaureate brand be likely to confer compared with its competitors; which countries would emerge in the next 10 years as the strongest International Baccalaureate growth points?

Where do you want your school to be positioned?

Having surveyed likely future scenarios:

- What do you want to strengthen?
- What is best abandoned altogether? (Organizations are not very good at deliberately abandoning something; instead they accumulate activities.)
- What new opportunities do you want to seize?
- What perils must you avoid?
- What size and shape do you want to be?
- What relationship do you want with your community?
- What distinctive characteristics do you want your school to have?

Set ambitious but straightforward goals—you are leading a school, not the United Nations—and you will find the very fact of defining these goals will take you halfway towards their achievement. You can now begin to measure the difference between where you will be if you do nothing, and where you really want to be. This is sometimes known as the "strategic gap".

Focus on strategic goals

Now you must seek to close that strategic gap by focusing on a limited number of strategic goals. In Geneva we chose six strategic goals in the areas of:

- education programmes
- special educational needs
- staff policies
- finance and resources
- governance and
- communication.

For the first International Baccalaureate strategic plan we chose eight goals and called them "*grandes lignes*"–the title came to me while waiting to catch a train at the Gare de Lyon in Paris, reflecting on the way France is held together by its impressive rail network. The McKinsey plan identified three overarching goals: quality, access and infrastructure.

Break each goal into objectives

Finally, each strategic goal must be broken down into a limited number of quite high-level objectives. At the International School of Geneva, for example, the broad strategic goal *To offer a world-class international education* was developed into six objectives related to:

- the international curriculum
- serving the whole person
- promoting innovation
- reinforcing languages
- reducing class size and
- evaluating the quality of education.

At this stage, the McKinsey International Baccalaureate strategic plan was expressed in terms of 28 strategic objectives. You have now reached the level that meshes in with the school's organizational structure and the responsibility for achieving these objectives can be appropriately assigned.

Put it into practice

So now you have your strategic plan. Well ... yes and no. What you have is a document that will either gather dust in your cupboard or else prove to be a blueprint for systematic, long-term improvement. What happens next will determine which it will be, because, however many committees, working parties and study groups may have contributed up to this point, the majority of the school's community will claim to know nothing about it. An effective strategic plan must be understood and owned by the entire organization, and that means challenging each of the school's different units—departments, year groups, teams—to set their annual objectives within each of the plan's strategic objectives. For example, exactly how is the Year 9 team of tutors going to contribute to the objectives under the strategic goal of "communication"? What annual objectives will they set that are Specific, Measurable, Achievable, Realistic and Timed (SMART) as well as accurately costed? Such unit responses are sometimes known as business plans, and it is at this point that the strategic plan begins to penetrate the fabric of the school.

The importance of working within the framework of a strategic plan was well illustrated by the decision to close the school's boarding houses in Geneva. This was an entirely rational decision: boarding was losing money; it represented a tiny fraction of the student population in a school whose ethos was that of a day school; we could realize a substantial capital gain; we had no wish to attract students expecting to "finish" their education in a smart, Swiss environment. What we forgot, however, was the strategic objective to create a system of scholarships to allow students from other countries to study at the school. Where were all these new scholars going to live? There are now plans to build a new boarding house.

A final word of warning

The process of cutting up a school into thinner and thinner slices, converting its mission statement into goals then strategic objectives and finally into business plans, runs the risk of reducing it to dozens of unrelated fragments. Someone—and it has to be the head in the role of chief story-teller—must be regularly doing the reverse process, piecing all the bits together to recreate the whole; reminding everyone what the mission is all about, what the journey is for.

T is for Transparency

Knowing something that someone else does not know makes you more powerful, and in choosing how to handle information—to transmit, distort or withhold it—the leader is in a very strong position to exert authority. You can imagine a membrane surrounding the head's office through which communication with members of the school's community (including its own employees) must pass. Is that membrane transparent? When they look at the school do they receive a clear image? Or is the membrane translucent, distorting the image to the head's advantage? Or is it opaque, completely obscuring the truth?

Let me share one of my more embarrassing professional experiences. Two parents, recently divorced after an acrimonious legal battle, have temporarily buried their differences to confront me with their combined fury. They are waving the school's confidential (as it was at that time) report written about their daughter for her art college application which a careless admissions tutor has actually handed to the student. So much for confidentiality! The parents are furious that the report refers to their divorce as a possible reason for their daughter failing to achieve her true potential in her forthcoming examinations. Their anger at reading about their personal dispute obscures the fact that it was written solely for their daughter's advantage. The school's transparency has become an invasion of the parents' privacy.

I remain unrepentant about that report—written by the head of sixth form but signed by me. The information was relevant, accurate and expressed in appropriate language; unfortunately, the parents saw something never intended for their eyes, but my conscience is clear. It does, however, raise the whole question of what information can reasonably be concealed or restricted. In practice, confidentiality is used as much as an excuse to flaunt authority as it is to restrict sensitive information. Nothing signals authority more powerfully than the ability to say "I can only tell you this in the strictest confidence ..." or, more tantalizingly, "I'm afraid what you ask is confidential." Of course, in practice it never does remain confidential so why not agree that very little information in schools need be concealed unless it is protected by legislation, relates personally to an individual (Does that include the divorce case? you might reasonably ask) or threatens security.

A t the International School of Geneva, where we had a number of very high-profile parents, we made the decision to refuse to confirm or deny that a particular child was even a student at the school. This fuelled regular and thoroughly entertaining media speculation about the President of North Korea, Kim Jong-il, who was rumoured to have been a former student. Well, who knows, perhaps he was ... or maybe he wasn't ...

As a general rule, though, we would do well to remember one of the British philosopher, Bertrand Russell's, "ten commandments for a teacher", proposed in his "A Liberal Decalogue":

Do not think it worthwhile to proceed by concealing evidence, for the evidence is sure to come to light.

This is even more likely to happen with access to the Internet and with an increasing amount of information about the school required, by law, to be made available on its website. It is now very difficult indeed to conceal the truth under the cloak of confidentiality, and it is therefore a good idea to be upfront with bad news.

I remember driving right to the other side of town in order to get my hair cut by someone who knew absolutely nothing about The Heathcote School – I always feel vulnerable when I am trapped in a barber's chair—but in vain. "I hear there was some trouble on the French exchange last week", said this complete stranger, in unnecessarily loud tones. Somehow he was ahead of me and I was immediately on the defensive. Today, with the benefit of a school website, the news of exactly what had happened in France and how it had been dealt with could have neutralized his pre-emptive and noisy strike.

All schools make mistakes, and I always urged my colleagues to build up a well of goodwill during the good times by going the extra mile with students and parents. Then, when the bad times come, as one day they will, you can admit your mistake and dip your bucket into the well. But you must never allow the reservoir to run dry. My message clearly got through, because when I left the International School of Geneva the staff gave me a pail as a memento!

With thought, and an attitude of transparency rather than concealment, potentially damaging situations can be turned to advantage.

The industrial action taken by teachers at The Cavendish School meant that communication with parents became very difficult. Normal parents' consultations were suspended so we started a special newsletter, ironically called *News from Somewhere* (I wonder if anyone made the connection with William Morris's utopian *News from Nowhere*). This developed into a regular form of communication once the industrial action was over and was efficiently managed by a dedicated group of parents.

Most of the mistakes in my career can be attributed to poor communication. I tend to assume that because *I* know, everyone around me must also know, so the careful process of reaching a decision is ruined at the last minute by its bungled communication. Maybe there was some excuse when informing others meant convening meetings, typing lengthy reports and distributing copies of minutes. Today, with all the electronic technology that is at our disposal, there is no excuse. Of course, this means acquiring new skills and techniques, such as chairing video and telephone conferences that are now an everyday part of communication in an international organization like the International Baccalaureate. Agendas need careful planning, decisions must be limited to a few key issues and protocols for participation in discussion have to be clearly explained and strictly maintained. In other words, it calls for tough chairing!

There is a legal framework that maintains transparency in a school: the regular reporting to parents, access to the minutes of important meetings, the statutory information available to the whole community, including inspection reports and standardized testing data. But this provides only half the picture. The other half must be described by the leader in the role of story-teller, seizing every opportunity to explain, illustrate and reinforce the purpose and the values of the school. I have tried to do this in all the obvious ways: introductions to parents' newsletters, a brief welcome at every parents' consultation, presentations on more formal occasions such as speech days and graduation and, of course, talking to the regular assemblies with the students.

If I were a school leader today I would be writing a weekly web log for the school's community. Blogging offers a wonderful medium for adding the unofficial subtext that helps to explain what the school is really like; you can make a sound link to last night's choir concert, add a video clip of the charity walk and invite interactive comment and discussion on a range of issues. This really does convey the message that the school has nothing to hide and you could even explain what really did happen on the French exchange.

U is for Unacceptable performance

It has been mutually agreed to let Mr Prendegast go. We are grateful for his contribution to the school and we wish him well in his new chosen career.

Don't believe a word of it. Mr Prendegast did not want to go and the shame he and his family feel about his departure will most likely undermine his health still further. No one is especially grateful to him for the regular mayhem that was a feature of his history lessons and, to be honest, the chances of his getting another job at the age of 59, never mind starting a new career, are about zero. Prendegast has been dismissed, sacked, fired.

As in all walks of life, incompetence is to be found in schools; indeed, it would be an unusual school whose head was not concerned about the poor performance of one or two colleagues. In contrast to some other walks of life, however, incompetence in schools is painfully and publicly apparent and personally shameful. Every time teachers go into a classroom, laboratory or workshop, they put their personalities on the line, and rejection is a humiliating experience. Never mind his performance as a history teacher; several times a day Mr Prendegast has been judged as a human being and he has been found wanting.

This acute sense of personal involvement, putting one's personality on the line, makes teachers very reluctant to admit their failure. Deep down they suspect that it is not their lack of preparation, their inadequate equipment or their inability to communicate: it is something to do with them, as a person, that is wrong, and that hurts. I have met very few teachers who were prepared to admit they had a problem; but I have met many who were very relieved when the deception was finally brought to an end.

But let us begin at the beginning. Every new employee signs a contract and so do you, as the employer, or the representative. Those two signatures denote a shared commitment to making the appointment a success; after all, in addition to the potential human commitment, the school has already incurred substantial advertising, interviewing and relocation expenses, so let us do everything possible to make this investment work. This means a comprehensive programme of induction, the assignment of a mentor or buddy, close supervision from the line manager and an early appraisal. It means giving praise where it is due and honest criticism when it is not. Criticizing a colleague is never easy, and its effectiveness usually depends upon timing. Rarely is it appropriate to react immediately the offence is committed; much better to wait for a moment of calm and a moment of formality when the employee is hearing as well as listening.

Let us suppose, however, that despite your best efforts, alarm bells are beginning to ring and you are playing that difficult game of trying to extrapolate present performance into the future. Is it a weakness of technique, which can be improved, or does the teacher lack some of those basic qualities that are fundamental to success:

- a respect for young people
- a lack of fear of young people and their sometimes disturbing behaviour
- the determination to be a model of competence
- the capacity to communicate and
- a sense of optimism about the future?

Most contracts will have an option of termination after three months, but this is usually invoked only in extreme situations; other cases that are more marginal are given the benefit of the doubt, and this is right, because for every person who subsequently fails there will be 10 others who will eventually succeed. The real worry, therefore, is less about early incompetence and more about the teacher's longer-term development.

After an initial period of a few years, it is usual for a contract to become open-ended: it no longer requires renewal. I know some schools that manage to keep their staff on a series of short-term contracts, but this leads to instability and is illegal in many countries. The key question now is what do you do about the mid-career teacher who has an unlimited contract and whose performance has become unacceptable. Once again, the first response must be to help in terms of advice and practical measures such as modifying the timetable, perhaps finding a more suitable room and giving better classroom support. A plan of action must be agreed with regular, clear deadlines, and you should now open a file on the employee in order to document every complaint and the action taken. This must be accessible to the employee and allow for a written response to your actions. In cases of this kind that I have inherited, only rarely have I found any documented evidence of dissatisfaction, still less the detailed "paper trail" that is needed to support subsequent tough action.

In the absence of improvement the most difficult decision will be to choose the moment to withdraw your support, having now decided that the contract must be terminated. I can now fully understand how a head of government pledges unqualified support for a senior minister one day and then sacks him the next. In public it has to be black or white; there can be no grey shades of doubt; the moment the community doubts the leader's support for a colleague, that person is doomed.

Unacceptable performance is often more difficult to resolve than unacceptable behaviour because it is usually subjective and often erratic: very rarely is the situation all bad all the time. In contrast, the teacher who forges his qualifications, or establishes an unacceptable relationship with a senior pupil, or regularly phones a sex chat-line while at work, or turns up drunk to a parents' meeting (I have experienced all these situations and more)—what the Swiss called *fautes graves,* serious errors—can be dealt with swiftly and decisively. But be careful: the drunk teacher may be in the early stages of alcoholism and there is nothing swift or decisive you can do about that. Indeed, much unacceptable performance has its roots in illness, and it is rarely the kind of illness that can be cured with staightforward keyhole surgery.

The pressures on teachers are enormous: to teach one really good lesson is a sufficient challenge, but to teach four or five different classes a day or to create structured learning from the potential chaos of a primary class every day, for weeks, months and years on end—that is the reality of this exhausting profession. You are in for a long haul dealing with colleagues suffering from stress, but if those bold words in the school's mission statement about "understanding" and "compassion" mean anything at all, they apply first and foremost to your own staff. This is a situation where subtle harassment, implanting feelings of guilt in the sick teacher, can all too easily influence your actions. Ask someone else to send the get-well-soon cards while you, the leader, adhere rigorously to the formal rules.

Meanwhile, Mr Prendegast has received his final written warning and yet another review of his lessons leads, with due notice, to the termination of his contract. His union representative is supporting him, on the one hand recognizing that it is in no one's professional interest to condone unacceptable performance, but on the other hand determined to ensure that the correct procedures are being followed. An appeal to the board of governors has failed and, on this occasion, you are unlikely to end up in front of an industrial tribunal, but if you do, so be it: you have played by the rules and you are acting in the best interests of the school. And at least Mr Prendegast knows the deception is over and he can look forward to some relief from the daily humiliation caused by his adolescent tormenters.

V is for Vision

"The first basic ingredient of leadership is a guiding vision"—so says Warren Bennis, my favourite writer on the subject, in his book *On Becoming a Leader*. But this statement worries me because the concept of a "vision" can be dangerously self-centred, even implying elements of religious conviction or extremist fervour. I have seen too many school leaders who were inclined to use their institution and the power they derived from it to promote a personal agenda. Their vision was very clear indeed, but it seemed to have more to do with their careers than with the future of the school for which they were responsible. To adapt an advertisement for a famous brand of Swiss watch, the head never owns the school; but looks after it for the next generation. The starting point is therefore the needs of the organization, not the visionary imagination of the leader.

I remember clearly in the early days of my first headship feeling a sense of guilt about my evident lack of missionary fervour. The school was not in crisis—far from it—and nothing needed immediately fixing. I simply wanted to retain the huge support of parents while introducing rather more transparency in our exchanges with them. I wanted to create conditions that would encourage the staff to continue to give of their best while helping some of them to embrace 20th-century rather than 19th-century pedagogy. I wanted to see if we could design a curriculum for this comprehensive school that would avoid an internal division into rapidly diverging grammar and secondary modern streams. None of this seemed to have much to do with a vision; on the contrary it all seemed rather pragmatic and down-to-earth.

Now, it is amazing what a difference a single word can make because, though I have doubts about "a vision", I have none whatever about "vision". Leaders certainly need vision that is (and here I quote my dictionary) imaginative insight, statesmanlike foresight and sagacity in planning. Essentially, it is the capacity to look ahead into an unknown future, to imagine what it will be like and to make decisions accordingly. As even the most powerful telescopes look into the past rather than the future, we do indeed have to use instead our imagination, foresight and sagacity. I can think of many issues, for example:

- the impact of information and communication technology
- the growing awareness of the true extent of special educational needs
- the increasing importance of raising extra funds
- the devolution of school budgets
- the centralization of the curriculum

all of which could have been anticipated by a leader with imagination, foresight and sagacity, that is to say with vision.

Crystal balls are unlikely to help much either, but a leader with vision (which, I insist again, is not the same as a visionary leader) can construct a personal radar system that scans the airspace and picks up signals from issues and events just coming over the horizon: an early warning system, if you like. The information that is fed into the system will come from several different sources, of which the school's own key performance indicators will be one, but I used to find my business and political contacts the most useful: they knew which way the wind was blowing long before the chill was felt in schools. The news was not always precise and rarely comforting (bad news travels much more quickly than good news), but it was usually worth taking seriously. I remember, for example, Sir Keith Joseph, then UK secretary of state for industry, telling me in the early 1980s, when Britain's economic situation was far from clear and manufacturing was in severe decline, "The whole of industry is in a thick fog. The only difference with ICI (the company with whom I was working at the time) is that they know they're in a thick fog." What he was not prepared to admit was his own responsibility for creating much of the fog.

At the International School of Geneva, the school's pension scheme was managed by the private bank, Lombard-Odier. Once a year the school's pension committee met at the bank to review with their experts the performance of our fund, one of the largest in Geneva. The meeting was followed by lunch accompanied by exquisite wines and then, over coffee, we were invited to sit back and listen to a wide-ranging analysis of the economic situation in Switzerland, Europe and the rest of the world. This was the Swiss playing their strongest game on their home ground and it was fascinating. Although I doubt if anything I learned during those lunches directly affected a decision I took back at school, they played a significant part in helping me to shape my vision of the future, to sharpen up the context in which decisions would be taken.

I must now return to my earlier dismissal of the visionary leader because on reflection this was perhaps a little premature. Let me approach the concept of "vision" from a different angle because this section might well have been titled "V is for Values". Now here we really do have something to be visionary about.

When I arrived at The Cavendish School I found it was known to the staff as "The Cavendish", which seemed to me just a little old-fashioned and curiously at odds with the many radical things the school was doing. However, I soon came to understand how this dichotomy, this split personality, was at the heart of the school's values: the one made the other possible. Thus, we had a close and formal link with the famous Cavendish Laboratory in Cambridge (known to generations of eminent physicists as "The Cavendish"): its senior administrator was an influential member of our board of governors. The school had introduced a most unorthodox science curriculum that had been welcomed by parents partly because of the sheer enthusiasm and commitment of the science teachers but also because the Cavendish Professor, Sir Nevill Mott FRS, had visited the school and said he liked it. My vision was to keep these two apparently contradictory, but in fact synergistic, conservative and reforming values in balance. They were what made the school distinctive.

At the International School of Geneva the school's values were made explicit in a formal charter that defined the activity of the school as being:

... based on the principles of equality and solidarity among all peoples and of the equal value of all human beings without any distinction of nationality, race, sex, language or religion.

In a school whose students came from more than 120 different nations, speaking more than 80 different mother tongues, that statement meant something; it mattered and it was regularly quoted to support or to challenge a particular line of action, as well as providing the bedrock of the school's strategic plan. Most of my public speeches, whoever was in the audience, would at some point, return to emphasize, reinterpret and explain that clear statement of basic values. The leader is a story-teller, responsible for maintaining but updating traditions and reminding the community about what the school stands for.

So Warren Bennis is right after all. **The school leader must have vision**: the capacity to imagine realistically what the future has in store. And **the leader must also have a vision** of a school that is able to face that future with confidence: a vision that is founded upon the values—intellectual rigour, compassion, open-mindedness and cultural understanding—that are the essential ingredients for a fulfilled life in the globalized society of the 21st century.

W is for Walking the talk

Mahatma Gandhi put it this way: "You must be the change you wish to see in the world." In other words, you, the leader, in the way you act and behave, must be the embodiment of the mission you are striving to achieve. Which sounds fine, but what does it actually mean; what do you have to do? Well, it does *not* mean stalking the corridors radiating leadership, nor does it mean interfering in tasks you have sensibly delegated to others. In order to grasp how the 21st-century phrase "walking the talk" really does translate into action, I am going to explore it from an unusual perspective: a 19th-century poem.

Leaving aside comic verse and limericks, I know of only one serious poem written about school leadership—and it is a blockbuster. In 1857, the English poet and critic Matthew Arnold looked back on the death of his father, the renowned headmaster of Rugby School, Thomas Arnold. Fifteen years had passed since Arnold senior had been buried in Rugby Chapel (the title of the poem), and his son had decided that it was time to re-establish his legacy. To do so he wrote a poem that is a wonderful description of educational leadership and of five different elements that make up "walking the talk":

- commitment
- participation
- optimism
- conciliation
- mission.

Commitment

The first quality—and remember that these qualities must be clearly visible to those around—is unswerving commitment and dedication to the task in hand. The poet contrasts true leaders

> *And there are some, whom a thirst*
> *Ardent, unquenchable, fires*

with those whose impact is no more than waves

> *Of the midmost Ocean, have swelled,*
> *Foam'd for a moment, and gone.*

Commitment in these terms, then, is an unquenchable thirst for the task in hand, which should not be confused with a mere enthusiasm or even a deep passion because, unlike those two, a thirst has to be satisfied if the leader is to survive. There is a compulsive element to leadership that cannot be switched off, even on a distant beach during the long weeks of the summer vacation. Unfortunately, it can slowly absorb the whole of your life.

Participation

Matthew Arnold's poem describes a journey through life; indeed, it describes two journeys. The first, in the mountains, starts well but the weather breaks and the group is soon in serious trouble

> *Cheerful, with friends, we set forth –*
> *Then, on the height comes the storm.*
> *Thunder crashes from rock*
> *To rock, the cataracts reply,*
> *Lightnings dazzle our eyes.*

The leaders struggle on and reach the safety of a lonely inn. But they soon realize that the rest of the party has been lost in the storm, swept away by an avalanche. This, says the poet, would never have happened with his father in charge. On the contrary:

> *Still thou turnest, and still*
> *Beckondst the trembler, and still*
> *Gavest the weary thy hand.*

So the second quality of walking the talk is never to lose contact with the rest of the group, especially when the going gets tough. Call it solidarity, call it mucking in, call it pulling together; the leader must remain in touch with the crowd, and sometimes there are unusual ways of doing this.

Optimism

Rugby Chapel opens on a gloomy November evening with the poet looking back to much earlier Novembers when the headmaster, Thomas Arnold, was still alive and his enthusiasm was dispelling the darkness:

> *In the gloom of November we pass'd*
> *Days not dark at thy side;*
> *Seasons impair'd not the ray*
> *Of thy buoyant cheerfulness clear.*

This public display of cheerfulness, optimism and hope is our third element of walking the talk. It is relatively easy to show leadership when the sun is shining and the visibility clear, but it is a different matter when the mists descend and a rocky shore is within earshot. Particularly difficult is to achieve the appropriate reaction on being given bad news. The last thing you want to hear on Friday afternoon is that bright-red painted graffiti has appeared all over the recently decorated toilets, so do you display anger, sympathy, resignation or nothing at all?

In practice, in those situations in which you are powerless, it is best to show solidarity with those who can do something and immediately invite the caretaker to show you what has happened. Action is always a good substitute for optimism.

Conciliation

So it is with optimism that the poet begins the second symbolic journey, not this time with a small group of friends in the Alps, but with humankind itself crossing the desert. Again, all is not well:

> *Factions divide them, their host*

> *Threatens to break, to dissolve.*
> *– Ah, keep, keep them combined!*
> *Else, of the myriads who fill*
> *That army, not one shall arrive;*

He could be describing a typical school staff room, and it illustrates the fourth of our qualities, namely the capacity to resolve differences and achieve public harmony. Most negotiation goes on in small groups, meeting in closed session, and the full staff meeting has acquired an unpopular image because it is rarely the most suitable forum for transacting specific business. Yet, if it is not the best meeting for reaching decisions, it is often the place where important areas of disagreement can be aired and the head's skills of negotiation and conciliation openly displayed. Walking the talk means feeling comfortable in the middle of very open disagreement and having confidence in your ability to bring about a greater sense of harmony.

Mission

At last the long poem ends, as the exhausting journey ends, on arrival at the chosen destination

> *Ye fill up the gaps in our files,*
> *Strengthen the wavering line,*
> *Stablish, continue our march,*
> *On, to the bound of the waste,*
> *On, to the City of God.*

Dr Arnold's educational mission had a clear goal, the preparation of Christian gentlemen, and he used every written and spoken opportunity to explain and expound it, particularly in his weekly sermons in the school chapel, from which his son deliberately borrowed phrases to use in the poem. The fifth and final quality, then, of walking the talk is the capacity to articulate the school's mission and to use appropriate means for doing so. Howard Gardner has suggested that one important driver for change is the number of different ways in which it can be explained: different minds respond to different stimuli. For most schools, chapel will not be an option, but there are many alternatives of which Thomas Arnold never dreamed.

The five qualities discussed above are those very public qualities that determine whether a leader can truly motivate and inspire. Even that later destroyer of reputations, the British writer and critic Lytton Strachey, wrote with some awe of Dr Arnold literally walking the talk in his mission to reform an educational system in which corruption and violence had become endemic:

> *As the Israelite of old knew that his almighty Lawgiver might at any moment thunder to him from the whirlwind, or appear before his very eyes, the visible embodiment of power or wrath, so the Rugby school boy walked in holy dread of some sudden manifestation of the sweeping gown, the majestic tone, the piercing glance of Dr Arnold.*

X is for Xenophobia

There is a sense of tribalism about a successful school and it is not easy for the leader to achieve the right balance between internal solidarity and external outreach. A good school is proud of its history; it is keen to establish its own culture and distinctive ethos; it often has its own motto and display cabinets filled with silver trophies. The wise head will be particularly sensitive to the importance of doing things the right way according to long-standing traditions.

At the same time, the school will probably be part of a wider educational grouping—a district or a local education authority—and it may have formed important partnerships with other local schools in order to make the most efficient use of expensive specialist resources. That means surrendering a measure of independence, perhaps contributing money and staff to a central pool. So these two forces—internal and external—pull in opposition and there is little doubt which is the more powerful. Consequently, many schools, sometimes the most successful schools, become inward-looking and even xenophobic, with a dislike or fear of strangers and strangeness.

Tribalism can cut off important messages from the outside world.

At The Heathcote School we had a very special relationship with the apprentice school at British Aerospace, and this encouraged me to propose an exchange between one of our teachers and one of their instructors. I use those different terms quite deliberately because I suspect the distinction made the whole arrangement illegal: the instructor, despite his obvious competence and enviable experience (he had worked on Concorde), was not a "qualified teacher". To their credit, for they must have had their suspicions, the teachers' union representatives did not blow the whistle and the exchange went ahead successfully. It had an unexpected outcome that was quite enough to justify the project: the teacher, whose speciality was technical drawing, realized that the subject, as he taught it, no longer existed outside school; it had been completely transformed by computer technology. What he was teaching was now the history of technical drawing.

Some years later, I wrote a report about a period of secondment I had spent with the chemical multinational, ICI, and I called it, tongue-in-cheek, "Isn't that rather commercial?" This was a phrase used by a colleague on hearing that I was about to spend several months supping with the devils of industry. Yet, looking back, it has been from those external contacts that have I learned about so many of the ingredients of leadership: 360° appraisal, job classification, psychometric testing and team building, for example. And it was to industry that I looked for a new and often refreshing stimulus in my work. I still remember the phone call from BAe one busy morning: "Are you by any chance free tomorrow? We have a spare seat on the plane for the Paris air show". Somehow, I managed to clear my crowded diary!

Schools are necessarily conservative institutions, but too often their tribal instinct encourages them to withdraw into the laager when something unfamiliar is spotted on the horizon. Or when some*one* unfamiliar is spotted, as at Carisbrooke High School, where the head had appointed an ex-naval officer as head of guidance and a priest as school chaplain—a unique situation for a state comprehensive school. Both appointments were viewed with some suspicion and succeeded only because of the strong personalities of the two incumbents and the unfailing support of the head. It is the school head who uniquely has the authority to destroy xenophobic tendency.

I am reminded of a moving incident in the classic novel *Goodbye Mr Chips* (whose quality is inversely proportional to its remarkable brevity). Mr Chips, finally appointed in old age to the acting-headship of Brookfield School, knows he will upset the school community when he includes Max Staefel, the former German master and now one of the enemy, in his weekly list of those killed fighting on the Western Front. Chips regrets how the qualities of dignity and generosity are becoming increasingly rare in a frantic world and adds, "Brookfield will take them, too, from me; but it wouldn't from anyone else."

This xenophobic tendency is further encouraged by the competitive environment in which most schools find themselves today, a situation encouraged by governments that believe that market forces should play an important part in deciding the future prospects of schools. Yet, in practice, many parents do not have a genuine choice of school so the overall quality of a school district is of paramount importance and heads must accept that they have a responsibility for the whole as well as the part which is their particular institution. It was this concern with the whole that led me to propose a merger of The Cavendish School with a neighbouring school.

The merger highlighted both the strengths and weaknesses of a school's tribalism. The school was proud to be different but, despite its liberal philosophy, it could sometimes be inward-looking; indeed, it was precisely to protect that liberal approach that it chose to look within. There was a much vaunted "Cavendish way", reinforced in a series of virtuous circles that touched every aspect of school life from assemblies to sports day. No opportunity was missed to emphasize the distinctive ingredients of a Cavendish education: a common curriculum, extensive mixed-ability teaching, a unique humanities course, integrated science, resource-based learning. It proved successful because we were not just committed to it, but obsessed by it, and the school was hugely popular. This made one aspect of the complex merger with the rather unpopular neighbouring school much easier: the amalgamated school would bear the successful name of Cavendish and would give more students the chance of a successful Cavendish education. Alas, it did not work out that way. The merger changed the socioeconomic balance of the intake of students upon which the ingredients had depended for their magic qualities. The Cavendish way had been developed within one very unusual school and had never been exposed to harsher conditions outside. When it was, it could not survive and the character of the school changed.

In Geneva I experienced another kind of xenophobia. The International School offered a bilingual education, but in practice each of its campuses was divided into Francophone and Anglophone sections and there appeared to be depressingly little contact between the two cultures. There was evident mutual professional respect, and in many cases close friendship, between the two groups of teachers, but I soon realized that the style of learning that each group was promoting was distinctly different. The French Cartesian logic was poles apart from the Anglo-American pragmatism. The Francophones seemed to be more formal, more didactic and less active and participatory in their learning than the Anglophones. What one group perceived as meticulous quality the other perceived as nit-picking tedium.

The solution seemed obvious, particularly in the context of an international school: a blend of the best of each tradition. But that misses the point because these traditions are core elements of their cultures and you cannot mix-and-match different components of a culture; you accept it in its entirety.

> Beware of jumping to simple conclusions: in Geneva it seemed obvious to the Anglophone science teachers that their Francophone colleagues were hopeless at practical science—they never seemed to carry out a single experiment with their pupils. So, to put them right a joint weekend's course of practical work in chemistry was organized, led by a British consultant. The Francophone teachers completed all the experiments with excellent results before the Anglophones had finished reading the instructions!

Y is for Yourself

Of all the advice that I have read as a head, the most encouraging comes from the American essayist Ralph Waldo Emerson, who wrote in 1841:

> *Insist on yourself; never imitate. Your own gift you can present every moment with the cumulative force of a lifetime's cultivation; but of the adopted talent of another, you have only an extemporaneous half possession.*

So there you are: just be yourself. But that reassurance brings with it a powerful responsibility to understand yourself and to understand how others perceive you. We are entering the realm of emotional intelligence, which determines our ability to manage ourselves and our relationships with others. As society has become more open, more democratic and therefore less tolerant towards personal abuse and harassment, the development of emotionally intelligent leaders has become a priority. Daniel Goleman, eminent US psychologist and organization consultant, has identified four fundamental capabilities for leaders:

- self-awareness
- self-management
- social awareness and
- social skill.

Each of these he has described in terms of a set of competencies. For example, empathy is a key competency of social awareness; communication is a key competency of social skill. Goleman has also studied the effectiveness of six different leadership styles—coercive, authoritative, affiliative, democratic, pacesetting and coaching—relating each to a different element of emotional intelligence, and he concludes that one of the hallmarks of a successful leader is the instinct to choose the appropriate style to suit a particular situation.

For me, the key word in that brief description is "instinct". Even in situations that allow the rare luxury of lengthy deliberation and extensive consultation, most judgments retain a significant element of "gut reaction". Can we exert any control over this instinctive element of leadership? How useful would it be to anticipate how we are likely to react to a given situation?

For me, it helps me to know that I am INTJ:

- I for Introvert
- often using N for iNtuition, while
- T for Thinking in a logical way and
- adopting a lifestyle based on rational J for Judgement.

I am now referring to the Myers–Briggs Type Indicator, which uses a set of psychometric tests based on the work of Carl Jung to measure one's natural style and preferences, identifying those actions which come easily, pleasurably and instinctively—in other words, the components of a gut reaction.

The Myers–Briggs Type Indicator (MBTI) helps you to understand yourself and your behaviour better because it describes your preferences in four areas: how you are energized, what you pay attention to, how you make decisions and the kind of lifestyle you prefer. My own profile of INTJ is quite uncommon in leaders (except, I am told, in Japan), and there are certain things I need to be aware of in what is described as a "Promethean" temperament. For example, I am likely to resent close supervision and control; I am likely to make others feel unnecessary or rejected; when I am tired I am likely to give way to outbursts of sharp verbal temper; at the end of a hard day's work I will probably want to go to bed when others want, indeed *need*, to socialize in the bar.

There is a whole industry of psychometric testing, but recent research has shown that these tests are not reliable predictors for making staff appointments. At the International School of Geneva, each of my senior colleagues took the necessary tests so that we could share our profiles and I think that knowledge of each other's preferences made us into a better team.

Recent work has cast doubt on the distinctive nature of the four MBTI categories (which were developed in the 1940s), and increasing attention is being paid to the so-called Big Five characteristics of personality:

- extroversion–introversion
- openness to experience
- conscientiousness
- agreeableness
- emotional stability.

The Big Five are deemed to be universal dimensions of personality, stable from about the age of 30 and heritable, at least in part, and only the first (extroversion–introversion) seems to overlap an MBTI category. But the Big Five have been criticized for not being independent of one another and lacking any underlying theory.

So we can argue over the detail, but I have nonetheless found the general concept very useful because it has alerted me to my preferences and to what comes naturally. I know that in order to behave differently and sometimes more appropriately, a conscious effort on my part will be required; it will not happen instinctively and I shall have to work at it.

Another model that I have found particularly helpful for raising my self-awareness in relation to those I work with, particularly the senior management team, is known as the Johari Window, a model developed in the 1950s. An imaginary window separates me from my colleagues and is divided into four panes through which knowledge about me can either pass, or be blocked.

- The **open pane** represents knowledge that is known both to me and to others, passing freely in both directions. This is essential for open, trusting relationships and effective communication.
- The **blind pane** represents knowledge about me that is known to others but not to me, so it is unidirectional and relationships are obscured. I am unaware of how others perceive me and therefore likely to be thick-skinned. Only if I can encourage appropriate feedback will I move some of this blind pane into the open pane, to permit more open, honest exchange.

- The **hidden pane** represents knowledge about me which I choose not to share with others; it is also unidirectional, but in the other sense and it requires disclosure on my part to move it to the transparent open window. How much about myself am I prepared to risk revealing?
- The **unknown pane** is perhaps the most intriguing part of the window. It represents that part of me that is yet to be revealed; neither I nor my colleagues are aware of it. What is it that uncovers hidden potential, sets new directions and opens up fresh opportunities? For me it is neither reading nor listening but rather being given the chance to do it. Throughout my career, those in authority have been prepared to take a gamble on my unexplored reserves because for no job did I have the exactly required mix of skills, qualifications and experience. Indeed, given the current tick-list obsession for matching people to posts, I doubt that I would now be appointed to any one of them. The only way to reveal the unknown is to take the risk that it exists and offer concrete opportunities to reveal it.

Leaders quickly find themselves in a rut of predictable responses, they are quickly known for the way they will react to a given situation. This is partly for self-preservation: the task is so demanding, so varied, so unpredictable from hour to hour that, simply to survive and retain one's sanity, some time must be spent on automatic pilot. But what so often makes the difference in a school is the leader's reaction to different human problems and, despite the volumes of rules, regulations and recommendations, this reaction is unavoidably programmed by the software of the leader's own personality. If you are going to "insist on yourself; never imitate", understanding yourself and how you are perceived by others is an essential part of your preparation for leadership.

Z is for Zest

At the end of each day—well, perhaps more realistically at the end of each week—you must go home with the feeling that, on balance, it has all been worthwhile. In a public sense that requires no effort from you because working in any field of education is deemed to be socially valuable, requiring no further justification on your part. But what about the inner, private and personal satisfaction? Has the week brought a keen sense of enjoyment and interest; a task that is relished; a job that brings zest? The inevitable frustrations and disappointments and the huge measure of personal stress that come with school leadership must be counterbalanced, indeed outweighed, not only by the satisfaction of professional achievement and a job well done, but—dare I suggest it—by a sense of fun. Alas, the word "fun" comes with socially irresponsible overtones, so instead I am suggesting a sense of "zest".

The school leader starts with two enormous advantages in building a zestful job. The first is the daily contact with students, with youth, with their challenging and sometimes bizarre ideas—quite simply with the future. Moreover, this contact is refreshed and renewed every year as the senior cohort leaves and a new, completely unknown, group of youngsters enters the school.

always chose to teach a first-year class and, while I do not believe that the heads need to establish their credentials by teaching a timetabled class, I do believe they should do it for the fun of it (there's that word again) and because the classroom, or in my case the laboratory, is one of the few places to offer temporary sanctuary from the telephone. I am not especially proud of the quality of my teaching as a head, and I leaned shamelessly on the support of the lab technicians as I arrived for my lessons slightly late, poorly prepared and with half my mind on a very different set of issues. Nonetheless, I tried hard to be a useful, if very part-time, member of the science department team, to support the head of department, to introduce the occasional new idea and generally contribute to thinking and development.

The second advantage is the head's prerogative to join in any of the school's activities. If done to excess, this quickly becomes resented as unwelcome interference but when all one's grand strategic plans have come crashing down by Thursday afternoon, there is much to be said for spending Friday morning helping to set out the tables in the examination hall or quietly stuffing reply slips into school report envelopes. And how many other jobs offer the opportunity to sing in the school choir, play in its orchestra, accompany a field trip and make a fool of oneself at the annual fête? But again, let's not overdo it to the point of self-indulgence; the zest comes from seeing others succeed in their roles, not in starring oneself.

When I was first interviewed for a headship, I was asked to describe the most important function of the job. "Creating the conditions for others to succeed," I replied rather smugly. I did not get the job. Today, I hope I would have rather more to say about how those conditions might be created, but the thrust of my answer would be broadly the same. Now, though, I also recognize that, in addition to the material benefits, resources and development opportunities that make a job professionally satisfying, there is another set of conditions that help to make it enjoyable. These include the hand-written thank-you notes for those who have gone the extra mile (to be used with discretion because this is a currency that quickly becomes devalued); the end-of-term glass of wine at The Cavendish School, invariably attended by the chair of the board of governors, who formally thanked everyone on behalf of the board—a simple but hugely appreciated gesture; the regular summer staff barbecues round the swimming pool at The Heathcote School; the Saturday morning bus from the International School of Geneva for the ski slopes in the nearby French Alps; in other words, the dozens of different ways that help to weld a school's staff into a mutually supportive and vibrant community. And when I say "staff", I mean all the staff, not just the teachers.

> When the International School of Geneva celebrated its 75th birthday, a village in the Valais, where we had sent students every year for field studies, offered a group free skiing for a day with lifts, instructors and lunch thrown in. But which group? I chose the staff of central finance and administration because they were hidden away in their own building and seemed to have little fun. We had a wonderful day together and, being Swiss, they beat me on every run.

Alas, the sun does not shine all the time and zestful leadership has to respond appropriately to the bad periods as well as the good. These will bring moments of shock such as a completely unexpected decline in the number of parents putting the school as their first choice. There will be moments of bitter disappointment such as finding an important sculpture that we had commissioned vandalized during the night and having to bring it inside the building for security: a significant defeat. There will be moments of tragedy such as the crash of Swissair's New York to Geneva flight SR111 that killed ten members of the school's community, leading to a depressing succession of funerals and memorial services. Zest implies energy rather than a forced cheerfulness and each of these situations—and many others besides—required immediate action rather than a sad, passive shake of the head. In every case there was work to be done.

But I cannot end this personal account of leadership on a note of sadness, on a *bémol* as the French would say, because that would totally misrepresent my own overall experience. Instead I return to the concept of fun, so unhelpfully defined in my dictionary as "sport, amusement, jocularity and drollery". No one is going to class the leadership of schools as a sport or an amusement, still less describe it as jocular or droll. Clearly, the official view would have us believe that fun adds no value whatever to the final product, yet it is fun that gets us up in the morning, and fun that keeps us fresh as we pursue a challenging profession that has no clearly definable outcome and brings measurable benefits only long after we are dead. So let me replace the two words that are in any case largely redundant in the English language—jocularity and drollery—by two that are very much alive and well—enjoyment and excitement. And this leads me to insist that serious fun, enjoyment and excitement, has its roots in intellectual stimulus, regular contact with interesting people and unpredictability.

As I look back over more than 30 years' experience of educational leadership I realize how each new day has brought fresh intellectual stimulus in the form of argument and debate, reading and writing, speaking and listening, challenging me to rethink my so-called area of expertise. I realize how each new day has brought me into contact with a variety of interesting people, particularly students, in dozens of different countries from Norway to South Africa, China to the United States. I realize how each new day, despite my increasing experience, has brought fresh challenges that I had never dreamt of. And if that is not described as fun then I am happy to settle for zest.

Glossary of terms

Assembly	A regular meeting of the school community or parts of it, usually with a moral or religious theme
Catchment area	The geographical area from which a school takes its pupils
Class tutor	The teacher responsible for the pastoral supervision of a group of students
Comprehensive school	A school that does not select students according to ability
CPD	Continuing professional development
Curriculum	The school's planned programme of learning
Faculty	The school's academic staff
GCSE	General Certificate of Secondary Education, subject-based examination usually taken at age 16
Grammar school	A secondary school that selects its students according to ability
Head of department	The teacher responsible for the administration of an academic department in a secondary school, e.g. "head of history"
INSET	In-service education and training

Glossary

Local education authority (LEA)	The unit of local government in the UK responsible for the administration of state education
Parent teachers association (PTA)	The informal organization that brings together socially a school's parents and teachers
Parents' evening	The formal consultation meeting between parents and teachers
Pastoral care	The school's provision for the personal welfare of its students
Period	A unit of teaching on a weekly timetable or schedule
Primary school	A school usually for students aged 5 to 11
Sabbatical	A period of professional absence (paid or unpaid) agreed by the school
Secondary school	A school usually for students aged 11 to 18
Secondary modern school	A secondary school attended by students who were not selected for a grammar school
Sixth form	The two final years of secondary education
Speech day	The annual public celebration of a school's achievements
Timetable	The weekly schedule of different lessons
Tutor group	A group of students that meet together for pastoral supervision

About the author

George Walker started his career in education as a science teacher and ended it as director general of the International Baccalaureate. In between he spent nearly 30 years in the leadership of schools, experience that forms the basis of this book. He was appointed OBE for his services to education and is visiting professor in the University of Bath.